# Friend Paul

Background Books 6

# Friend Paul

*His Letters, Theology*
*and*
*Humanity*

*by*

*Neal Flanagan O.S.M.*

**Michael Glazier**
Wilmington, Delaware

## About the Author

Neal Flanagan, O.S.M., was trained in Pauline studies by Stanislas Lyonnet at the Pontifical Biblical Institute in Rome and by Pierre Benoit at the Ecole Biblique in Jerusalem. He was Professor of New Testament Studies at the Graduate Theological Union, Berkeley, from 1972 until his death in 1985.

First published in *Background Books* in 1986 by Michael Glazier, Inc., 1935 West Fourth Street, Wilmington, Delaware, 19805. ©1986 by Michael Glazier, Inc. All rights reserved. Library of Congress Card Catalog Number: 85-45554. International Standard Book Number: 0-89453-541-2. Cover design by Brother Placid, OSB. Printed in the United States of America.

# Contents

72659

*TO LARRY AND LORETTA SARAHAN*
*TO KATHLEEN AND FRANK*
  *ELLEN AND TOM*
    *NEAL AND JOYCE*
      *TERESA*
          *MICHAEL AND MARIA*
          *PAUL*
            *LORETTA*

*WHO HAVE—*
  *FOR SO LONG*
  *AND IN SO MANY WAYS—*
*LIVED THE DEATH AND RISING*
*OF THE LORD.*

# Preface

You can love Paul, you can hate him; you can trust Paul, you can feel uneasy in his presence. The one thing you cannot do as a Christian is ignore him. Paul is just too important for that. Centuries go by, civilizations change, nations rise and fall, reformations occur, new Church Councils and Church organizations appear, problems change—and, somehow or other, Paul and his writings always seem to be the center of inspiration and attack and defense and confirmation. It is this fact that consents to the appearance of yet another book on Paul and his creative concepts regarding God and Jesus and humankind.

The audience visualized for *Friend Paul* includes any and all persons interested in Paul's Christian theology, in the God-meaning that this extraordinary Jewish Christian finds in the life, death, resurrection and exaltation of Jesus of Nazareth, Paul's risen Lord. Though these pages found their birthing audience in classes of women and men preparing for the ministry, it is hoped that they will be serviceable also for less highly-powered lay people seeking a deeper understanding of the meaning of both Christ's life and their own. There is no reason for believing that Paul's thoughts were so baffling or bizarre that they can't be translated into easily comprehensible ideas and language. And even more important than understanding Paul is getting to know him as a personal friend and making his thoughts and goals part of one's own inner dynamism. This, too, *Friend Paul* hopes to help accomplish.

The Scripture quotations—unless otherwise noted—come from the Revised Standard Version. Suggested readings can be found at the end of each chapter. These are, of necessity, both limited and subjective. Readers are encouraged to add on to these as other pertinent articles and books come their way in future years.

# 1

# Introductory Material

This chapter hopes to provide, in brief form, material which will serve as an introduction to Paul, his life and his writings. The selection of topics is necessarily subjective, but the intent is to draw the reader into the immediate context of Paul, to be reminded of his life and works, and to begin a personal dialogue with a man whom no Christian can afford to ignore. Once the introductory material has been treated, we will move directly into the Pauline letters, treating all of them except the Pastorals.

## 1. NUMBER OF PAULINE LETTERS: THEIR ORDER

The books of the New Testament which make claim to Pauline authorship total 13. As ordered in all Christian bibles, these brief writings are Romans, 1-2 Corinthians, Galatians, Ephesians, Philippians, Colossians, 1-2 Thessalonians, 1-2 Timothy, Titus and Philemon. There is considerable discussion as to whether Paul actually wrote all 13. Three of them, 1-2 Timothy and Titus, the Pastoral Letters, provide serious evidence of having originated from a different source. A large group of scholars challenge Paul's authorship of Ephesians; a less substantive number raise doubts with regard to Colossians and 2 Thessalonians. This leaves a solid block of 7 writings which constitute a Pauline island protected by the moat of almost universal scholarly acceptance. Hebrews makes no claim to Pauline authorship, and it would be difficult, if not impossible, to find any reputable scholar who would make such a claim today.

The order of the Pauline literature found in our bible is not chronological. It is determined by the length of the writings—thus Romans comes first—and by setting the letters to the churches before the four letters addressed to individuals (1-2 Tim, Titus, Philemon). The following graphic is illustrative of the way Pauline scholarship views the closeness of the various writings to the heart and core of Paul's theology. The Pastorals lie in the outer circle, *Pauline* but not by Paul. The inner circle includes 1-2 Cor, Gal and Romans. 1 Thess (and quite possibly 2 Thess also), Philippians, and Philemon have indisputable Pauline characteristics and stand next to the inner circle. Colossians and Ephesians, if Paul's, mark a striking evolution in Paul's thought.

## 2. CATEGORIES FOR LETTERS

There are a number of different ways to categorize sections of the Pauline literature.

a) The *Great Letters* is a name often given to the central core of 1-2 Cor, Rom and Gal.

b) The *Captivity Letters* are those which allude to an origin from prison. These are Phil, Phm, Col and Eph.

c) The three *Pastorals* are so called because they suppose Paul's pastoral advice to his fellow-workers Timothy and Titus.

d) Four letters (1-2 Tim, Tit, Phm) are addressed to *individuals*.

e) The remaining nine letters are addressed to *churches*.

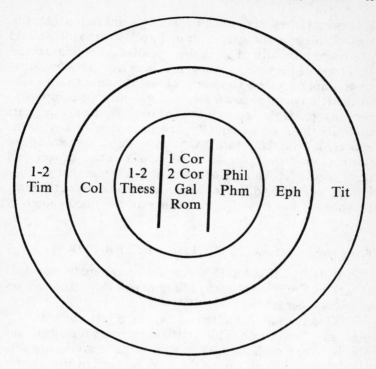

## 3. LETTERS OR EPISTLES?

Whether we judge Paul's writings to be letters or epistles depends on our definition of terms. A "letter" generally supposes a personal quality, a rather informal communication between individuals or groups usually bonded to some degree in friendship. An "epistle" generally bears a formal quality and can often be equated to a scholarly tract, treatise or essay. If these descriptions be taken as somewhat adequate, Paul's writings are, to a great extent, letters rather than epistles. They are usually written to people whom Paul knows and loves, occasioned either by some personal problem to which Paul responds or by Paul's wish to fill the void of his absence with at least the consolation, guidance and challenge of his written word. It is also true, however, that these Pauline letters can come close, at times, to the essay form. Romans, for example, though filled with intensely personal passages, is a well-crafted treatise, the greater part of which Paul could equally well have sent to any of his churches. Ephesians, too, if written by Paul, has exchanged the personal touch for an outflow of effusive prayer and deep theology. And all of the writings, even that to Philemon, intend to address churches as a whole. Even the most personal of Paul's writings visualize an extended audience.

## 4. CONSEQUENCES OF THE LETTER FORM

If it be true that Paul's letters are, in the main, personal letters to Christian friends, a number of important consequences emerge.

a) One is that, in the letters, we have just one side of a dialogue, Paul's side. This limits, sometimes seriously, our ability to comprehend the situation. Paul is giving answers to questions which are not visible, and often the answer would be so much clearer if we only knew what the original problem was. This difficulty is particularly pronounced in a "problem letter" such as 1 Corinthians. What questions or problems lie behind 1 Cor 7? Is Paul responding to Christians who advocate universal celibacy, in which case he is encouraging moderation in such an attitude? Or does Paul feel that he must encourage virginity whenever possible for Christians living in a sexually permissive society? The ambiguity of such one-sided conversation leaps out at us in a statement such as Col 4:17's "See that you fulfill the ministry which you have received in the Lord." Of what ministry does Paul speak in these words addressed to Archippus? And what is Paul speaking about in 1 Cor 11:34's "About the other things I will give directions when I come"? This lack of knowing the other side of the discussion sets limits to the depths to which we can penetrate Paul's advice.

b) Another important consequence to the fact that Paul wrote his theology in letters—as a pastoral theologian, therefore—is that he himself never organized his thinking into one master presentation. He was not, in today's jargon, a systematic theologian. What he writes in one section must be balanced by what he writes in another. His emphasis when speaking of *this* pressing problem must be weighed against a different emphasis under different conditions. Although it seems necessary for each of us to attempt some unification and organization of "Pauline theology," we do this with a certain risk. What might seem of importance to Paul's thinking, e.g. the "veil" in 1 Cor 11, would hardly have appeared at all if Paul had ever written his own Summa Theologica or Principles of Christian Belief.

c) As letters, Paul's writings are not restricted to teaching. They do teach, certainly, but intend much more than that. Like a good sermon, of which they are Paul's written substitutes, they purpose also to encourage, to reprove, to improve. Hearing them read aloud, as they surely were in the Pauline churches, can give us a clearer feeling of Paul's purpose and of the emotions with which he speaks and which he intends to arouse. Many passages of these letters permit us to still hear in the twentieth century the living voice of the apostle.

d) Last, but not least, the character of a personal letter demands that not all the content be of equal value. As Paul responds to church problems and personal questions, he does not have complete control over the situation. Questions are asked at times which were of significance—not necessarily great—to someone or some group in the first century, but which are of little or no significance today. This fact, which flows from the very nature of personal, occasioned letters, gives us ground to distinguish between the TIMELY and the TIMELESS in Paul's statements. This, surely, is not an easy task, but it is often enough a necessary one. The veil problem of 1 Cor 11 is, again, an outstanding example. Surely Paul would not have included this material if it were not among "the matters about which you wrote" (1 Cor 7:1). Paul *had* to deal with the question because it concerned what definitely was a problem for some Corinthian Christians. And, after working through a theological approach (vv. 7-12), and a law of nature approach (vv. 13-15) he finally turns to a simple sociological solution, the traditional practice of the churches (v. 16). Clearly we have here not timeless theology but what Paul at that time considered good practical advice. The timely, rather than timeless, character of this passage has been acknowledged by the presence of unveiled women in all the Christian churches of this century. If all of Paul's admonitions are equally timeless in quality, back into the veil go Christian women!

## 5. LITURGICAL USE IN THE PAULINE CHURCHES

There are clear indications in the letters that Paul intended that they be read in the Christian assemblies gathered for worship in the name of the Lord. In what is probably the earliest Pauline letter which we possess, Paul states strongly, "I adjure you by the Lord that this letter be read to all the brethren" (1 Thess 5:27). The most, or only, logical time for such a gathering would be at the eucharistic assembly. Col 4:16 supposes the same practice: "And when this letter has been read among you, have it read also in the church of the Laodiceans..." This introduction of Paul's writings into the context of the eucharist where, following Jewish worship practice, there would also be the reading of the Torah and the other sacred books was the first step toward the eventual canonization of the Pauline letters. Christians were led in a very practical fashion to equate Paul's writings to those of Moses and the prophets. And the divine inspiration which was presumed for the Jewish sacred writings was thus recognized as also present in those of Paul. The culmination of this process is seen clearly in 2

Peter 3:15-16: "So also our beloved Paul wrote to you according to the wisdom given him, speaking of this as he does in all his letters. There are some things in them hard to understand, which the ignorant and unstable twist to their own destruction, as they do *the other scriptures.*" Here Paul's letters are equated to the other scriptures of the Jewish people, now become the common property of Christians as well.

## 6. APPROXIMATE DATES OF PAUL'S LIFE

The chronology of Paul's life can be determined only in broad terms. Precise information is scanty. The one key date is determined by Paul's encounter with Gallio in Corinth (Acts 18:12-17). From outside sources we know that Gallio was proconsul in Corinth between 51-52 AD. This permits us, working backwards, to date the Council of Jerusalem (Acts 15:1-29; Gal 2:1-10) to c. 50 AD. Further back-tracking leads us to a period seventeen years before (Gal 2:1 plus Gal 1:18) to Paul's conversion to Christ c. 33 AD. If, as Acts 7:58 indicates, Paul/Saul was a young man at the time, his birth must have been in the very earliest years of the Christian era.

According to Luke's account in Acts, the Council of Jerusalem was preceded by Paul's missionary journey into Asia Minor and followed by the two trips which moved the gospel into Macedonia, Greece, and across to Ephesus and the territory under its influence.

All agree that Paul died in the sixties, either at the end of the Roman captivity indicated in Acts 28:30 or a few years later at the end of a second Roman captivity. Thus, an approximate calendar of Paul's life would be:

| | |
|---|---|
| birth | - c. 1 AD |
| conversion to Christ | - c. 33 |
| 1st visit to Jerusalem | - c. 36 |
| 1st missionary journey | - few years before 50 |
| Council of Jerusalem | - c. 50 |
| Gallio in Corinth | - 51-52 |

two missionary journeys
into western Asia
Minor, Macedonia
and Greece                  - c 50-58
imprisonment in
Jerusalem and Caesarea    - 58-60
death in Rome             - c. 62 or 66

This loose dating allows us to divide Paul's life into two fairly equal sections, that of Saul the zealous Jew (1-33) and of Paul the zealous Christian (33-66).

## 7. CHRONOLOGICAL RELATIONSHIP TO THE GOSPELS

With few exceptions, scripture scholars agree that Paul died before the appearance of any of our four canonical Gospels. His death in the sixties antedated the publication of Mark's Gospel, almost universally dated to about the year 70. Paul's frequent use of the word "gospel" as either a noun or verb refers to its root meaning, the "good news." The word had not yet been limited to its later use as descriptive of the written texts produced by the four evangelists. The fact that Paul wrote the earliest extant pieces of Christian literature means that for his writings he had no Christian bibliography to fall back on. Paul's sources were the oral tradition dating back to Jesus and based on the memories of the Twelve (Gal 1:18-19), certain revelations (2 Cor 12:1-7) and Paul's conversion encounter, and Paul's own creative theological genius, aided, as he himself believed, by the presence of the Spirit (1 Cor 7:40; 2:16).

## 8. LITERARY FORMAT OF PAUL'S LETTERS

Letters, like many other literary forms such as contracts, invitations, birth and death notices, want-ads and book reviews, develop a common pattern. It would be rare, striking and probably significant if we were to begin and end a letter without a gracious introduction and conclusion. Letters in Paul's day were also of uniform design, with an introduction and conclusion framing the actual body or central message. Frequently they were short notes, limited to the size of a small papyrus sheet. Paul's letters follow the same basic pattern, but with a few added characteristics. His *introduction* included references to both God and Christ. This was followed ordinarily by a *thanksgiving*. Frequently the *body* of the letter emphasized some doctrinal content, and was followed by a moral *exhortation* to Christian living. The *conclusion* was also phrased in Christian terminology. This, then, is the framework of a Pauline letter:

a) introduction;
b) thanksgiving;
c) body;
d) exhortation;
e) conclusion

Paul, however, was not captured by the frame. He remains quite capable of eliminating a section—as he does the thanksgiving in Galatians—or of merging doctrine with moral exhortation.

It is impossible to determine the influence of Paul's letter writing upon later Christian authors of the first century AD, but it is striking that all subsequent N.T. writings—with the exception of the Gospels, Acts and Apocalypse—are in the form of letters and bear at least a broad resemblance to Paul's communications.

## 9. SECRETARIES

Paul tells us clearly in his letters that he made frequent—if not constant—use of secretaries. In 1 Cor 16:21; Gal 6:11; 2 Thess 3:17; Col 4:18 we are told that Paul now concludes in his own hand. What precedes, therefore, was written by another. In Rom 16:22 the secretary himself rises from the text: "I, Tertius, the writer of this letter, greet you in the Lord." Although Tertius is the only secretary thus identified by name, it may be that others of Paul's scribes appear in the greetings which initiate the letters. Possibilities, therefore, are people like Silvanus and Timothy in 1-2 Thess, Sosthenes in 1 Cor, and Timothy again in Phil and Colossians. Another possibility is Tychicus who appears in Col 4:7-9 and Eph 6:21-22 as Paul's letter bearer and personal messenger. Epaphras of Col 1:7-8; 4:12 is another candidate. Himself the founder of the Church at Colossae (Col 1:7), and present with Paul during the composition of the letter (4:12), he must have been involved in some creative fashion in Paul's words to this Church with its unusual problems.

That Paul used secretaries is an established fact. How, and to what extent, he used them are unanswered questions. If he dictated, the secretary served simply as Paul's controlled instrument, relaying Paul's message word for word. If, however, Paul always, or on occasion, gave freedom to the secretary to express Paul's thoughts in the secretary's own words, then slight differences in the Pauline terminology and composition technique are to be expected.

## 10. THE PROCESS OF WRITING

The physical process of writing at Paul's time was, to say the least, arduous. Writing was done ordinarily on either parchment, i.e. worked leather, or papyrus, thin slices from the papyrus plant glued in horizontal fashion on a backing of strips placed in vertical form. Neither parchment nor papyrus provided the smooth surface guaranteed us by modern paper. The pen was a split reed or quill, and the ink a composite of such material as carbon and glue or gum. This combination of parchment/papyrus, reed pen and intractable ink made writing a slow and difficult process, usually accomplished only by professional scribes. Modern students vary in estimating the time consumed in the actual process of writing, but the following description is representative.

"The physical act of writing letters like those of Paul was a long and heavy labor which we find it hard to imagine today. Apart from the mental effort of crystallizing difficult and subtle concepts and phrasing them adequately, the length of the text alone required several days' writing. But since Paul probably devoted only the hours of the evening or the nighttime to his letters...and since a scribe ordinarily could not work more than two or three hours at a stretch (he wrote crouched on the ground and holding the paper on a tablet in his left hand), we must conclude that ordinarily Paul's epistles were in the writing several weeks...

If we suppose that Paul, as is very likely, used the hieratic papyrus, he could get about 140 words on each sheet. Various references in ancient authors indicate that it took about one minute to write three syllables and an hour for seventy-two words. Naturally, these figures are approximate, but taking them as the average and as a basis, we find that the earliest epistle, *1 Thessalonians* which was 1472 words, must have taken ten sheets of papyrus and more than twenty hours' writing time. The longest epistle, that to the Romans, which contains 7101 words, required fifty sheets and more than ninety-eight hours' writing time. The shortest, the note to Philemon, required almost three sheets and more than four hours" (Ricciotti, *Paul the Apostle*, 145-146).

If this description is at all close to being accurate, it means that Paul's letters were written, not over a period of hours but of days or weeks. This must have resulted, as it does for us, in evident changes of mood, emotions and interests within an individual letter. Is this what has happened, for one example, in Phil 3:1-2 where what looks like Paul's intention to bring the letter to a close is followed by the unexpected introduction of a totally different topic? The Pauline letters must be filled with such inconsistencies.

## 11. PAUL'S KNOWLEDGE OF THE EARTHLY JESUS OF NAZARETH

The question of Paul's knowledge of Jesus of Nazareth is fascinating. One initial fact is certain: if our only knowledge of Jesus were to be found in the Pauline letters, we would know very little about the earthly life, of him whom we Christians worship as risen Lord and Son of God. It is this fact that has induced some scholars to believe that Paul had little knowledge of, and little interest in, the human son of Mary. As proof, they point both to the absence of information about Jesus in Paul's letters and to his own blunt statement: "From now on therefore we regard no one from a human point of view; *even though we once regarded Christ from a human point of view, we regard him thus no longer.* Therefore, if anyone is in Christ, he is a new creation; the old has passed away, behold, the new has come" (2 Cor 5:16-17). A study of Paul's writings, life story and theology, however, points in a different direction.

a) First of all, the citation from 2 Cor 5:16-17 does not indicate Paul's lack of interest in the human Jesus. The "human point of view" does not qualify a Jesus in whom Paul has no interest but qualifies Paul's way or manner of knowing. Just as he wishes to *regard no one* from a human point of view, so too does he now consider Christ from, or with, a viewpoint directed and enriched by the Spirit.

b) Paul *must* have known a good deal about Jesus' words and deeds. He, himself, tells us of a two-week stay with Peter. "Then after three years I went up to Jerusalem to visit Cephas, and remained with him fifteen days" (Gal 1:18). What did they speak about? Can one imagine, even in jest, that a man of Paul's insatiable curiosity spent most of the time speaking about the weather and the crops? It is more than probable that Paul drained Peter dry of his knowledge of Jesus.

He must also have known well the traditions of the Church of Antioch for which he worked so vigorously (Acts 11:26; Gal 2:11). There is no way that Paul could have worked with the Antiochean catechumens without knowing the basic facts about the life and teaching of the Nazarene.

Even Paul's (Saul's) pre-conversion persecution of Christians demands some knowledge of the Jesus story. One doesn't persecute the totally unknown. "For you have heard of my former life in Judaism, how I persecuted the church of God violently and tried to destroy it" (Gal 1:13). Luke, on his part, places Paul in close union with the chief priests in Jerusalem, the very authorities involved in Jesus' death (Acts 26:9-10).

c) And, in fact, Paul does give us some facts regarding Jesus' life. He knows that Jesus was born of woman, born Jewish (Gal 4:4), a descendant of David (Rom 1:3). He knows, and can express in what is already traditional language, the account of the Last Supper and the institution of the Eucharist (1 Cor 11:23-25). He knows—again in the language of tradition—the story of Jesus' death, burial, resurrection and appearances (1 Cor 15:3-5). He even knows of Jesus' relatives (1 Cor 9:5) and, specifically, of James (Gal 1:19; 2:9, 12).

d) Nor is Paul ignorant of Jesus' teachings. When faced with problems from the churches, he is quite capable of producing Jesus' instructions as a solution. He does this in 1 Cor 7:10-11 when questioned about divorce and the indissolubility of marriage. He does it also in 1 Cor 9:14 with regard to missionary payment; in 1 Thess 4:15 concerning the parousia; in Rom 14:14 where he declares all food clean.

e) There are, moreover, numerous Pauline texts which appear to be allusions to Jesus' teachings as recorded in the Gospels. The following are *some* of the possibilities:

| | |
|---|---|
| Rom 12:14 "Bless those who persecute you; bless and do not curse them." | Mt 5:44 "love your enemies and pray for those who persecute you." |
| Rom 13:8-10 "Owe no one anything, except to love one another; for he who | Mt 22:39-40 "And a second is like it. You shall love your neighbor as yourself. On these |

loves his neighbor has fulfilled the law...Love does no wrong to a neighbor; therefore love is the fulfilling of the law."

two commandments depend all the law and the prophets.

Rom 14:13 "Then let us no more pass judgment on one another."

Mt 7:1 "Judge not, that you be not judged."

Rom 14:14 "I know and am persuaded that nothing is unclean in itself."

Mk 7:15 "...there is nothing outside a man which by going into him can defile him."

Rom 16:19 "I would have you wise as to what is good and guileless (akeraious) as to what is evil."

Mt 10:16 "...so be wise as serpents and innocent (akeraioi) as doves."

1 Cor 4:2 "Moreover it is required of stewards that they be found trustworthy."

Lk 14:42 "Who then is the faithful and wise steward whom the master will set over his household..."

1 Thess 5:2 "For you yourselves know well that the day of the Lord will come as a thief in the night."

Mt 24:42-43 "Watch therefore, for you do not know on what day your Lord is coming. But know this, that if the householder had known in what part of the night the thief was coming, he would have watched and would not have let his house be broken into."

1 Cor 10:27 "Eat whatever is set before you."

Lk 10:8 "...eat what is set before you."

It is evident, even from these few examples, that Paul was a recipient of Jesus' teachings in formulas very similar to those shared by the first three evangelists, especially by Matthew and Luke. Though he may never have seen Jesus' words in any written form, he knew them—to an extent we cannot measure—from the oral tradition shared by all Christians of those early decades.

f) Yet, granted a certain amount of knowledge which Paul possessed about the life and teachings of Jesus of Nazareth, the material which forms the core of the Gospels, the question still remains legitimate: Why does Paul make so little use of Jesus' life and teachings? Why are the Pauline letters so different in content from the Gospel writings which appeared in the following 20-30 years? Answers are not difficult to find.

First, Paul's letters are indeed, *letters* and not Gospels. Written to committed and instructed Christians, and occasioned by events in the various communities, they demanded little or no mention of Jesus' life and teachings. Paul's letters are not directed to catechumens who needed the initial instructions of the Gospels, nor are they Paul's presentation of the broad sweep of Christian knowledge. They are, rather, responses to communities and individuals. Their content, therefore, is controlled by the events and personages that occasioned them. Yet, when problems like divorce or eucharistic abuses occur, Paul has Jesus-information at hand to help form his response.

Second, though Paul is adamant regarding his personal knowledge of the risen Lord (1 Cor 9:1; Gal 1:11-16), in all probability he had not known the historical Jesus. This placed him at some disadvantage with regard to Jesus' first followers, and Paul's relative silence may be a sign of this discomfort.

Third, and most important, Paul's approach to Jesus and to his own Christian audience was eminently existential. There is little or no insistence on the *past* for the past's sake. There is surely more insistence on the *future*. And there is tremendous insistence on the *present*. Paul was interested in what Jesus means to us now, and in the factors that make him live, or come alive, for us. Paul was not nearly so interested in giving information about Jesus' past, as in plugging his fellow Christians into the *present* life of the glorified Lord. For Paul, the existential, reaching-out-to-us-now elements of Jesus' life were his death, resurrection and the effusion of the Spirit. It is on these that Paul insists, almost exclusively. Paul divides his story of Christ into a pre-existence of the Son of God, a past existence of the historical Jesus, and a postexistence of the risen Lord. It is in Jesus' postexistence as glorified and glorifying Lord that Paul is especially interested.

## 12. PAUL'S CONTRIBUTION TO CHRISTIANITY

Paul's importance for Christianity, while impossible to estimate on any known scale, is also almost impossible to exaggerate.

Geographically speaking, Paul was deeply involved in the spread of Christianity from Jerusalem, heart and symbol of the Jewish world, across Cyprus and Asia Minor, through Macedonia and Achaia, and on to Rome, center of the Gentile world. His letters are addressed to burgeoning churches in these regions. Paul has been called the "midwife of Christianity" and the term is quite apropos. *Saul*, at the age of c. 33, entered into a group of Jesus' followers which centered around Jerusalem. *Paul*, at the age of c. 66, died in Rome as the leading missionary of what had now become a Church spread throughout the whole of the vast Roman empire. It is not that this expansion was all Paul's doing. He alone was fortunate enough to have had Luke to tell his story. Others entered into the work, too, but there is no doubt that Paul was outstanding. Saul entered in a barely identifiable group; Paul helped mightily to form this group into an international Church.

Theologically speaking, Paul's contribution to Christian theology, to the comprehension of the meaning of Christ, is almost incredible. No matter what the theological question over the centuries, Paul seems to provide either a direct personal response, or the elements for one. He and his writings are simply unavoidable as Christians search for a deeper understanding of their life in Christ. Paul is an unfailing companion as we attempt to understand the nature and personality of Jesus, his relationship to Yahweh, the meaning of his death, the sacraments of baptism, eucharist and matrimony, the structure and life of the Church which is Christ's Body, the power and effect of Jesus' resurrection, the importance of faith and the gifts, the significance of the new Adam and the Israel of God, and the principles of a moral life. Though Paul was never a systematic theologian, it is hard to dispute the claim that he was, and remains, the first and the most profound of all Christian theologians.

## 13. PAUL AS A FIGURE OF CONTROVERSY

Perhaps it was precisely because Paul was such an amazing theological thinker that he and his teachings have always been at the center of controversy.

a) During Paul's lifetime he was very much an "odd man out" to the recognized centers of authority. To the Jewish authorities, who had been the companions and inspiration of his early years, the Christian Paul was an apostate, a heretic. His claim of messiahship and divine sonship for a condemned and crucified criminal was, when judged against Deuteronomy 21:22-23, an act of blasphemy. His identification with the Gentiles and his cavalier treatment of the law put him outside the pale of Judaism. The "forty lashes less one" (2 Cor 11:24) with which he was beaten on five different occasions are crude testimony to the sharp break in relationship between Judaism and this wayward son.

With the strongly Jewish Church of Jerusalem, Paul's relationship was only slightly better. Paul was far too quick-moving, too progressive, too out-in-front. Where the Jerusalem Christians were still very much an active—though special—part of local Judaism, involved in Jewish prayers and feasts and temple and Law, Paul was known and rumored to be almost a Gentile, living and consorting with Gentiles, spreading a doctrine of salvation in which temple, synagogue and Law were non-essential. Every return to Jerusalem was, for Paul, a time of nervous personal anxiety; every return necessitated personal defense. Little wonder that he asks for the prayers of the Roman Christians as he plans what proves to be his final trip to the Jewish capital (Rom 15:31).

b) During the second century AD, Paul and his writings were forced into controversy by Marcion, who claimed that only the Pauline letters—which described the Law as the cause of sin (Rom 7)—and an expurgated version of Luke's Gospel were truly scripture. This native of Pontus, who came to Rome c. 140 AD and formed part of a fringe Christian group there, was convinced that the implacably just and wrathful God whom he found in the Jewish writings was not the God revealed by Jesus, and that the Christian Church should cut all ties with Judaism and its scriptures. The Church reacted strongly against Marcion. He was condemned by the Christian authorities in Rome and his brief canon declared insufficient as the Church itself was thereby moved into the process of determining in detail precisely what the sacred scriptures should include. But Marcion's strong advocacy of Paul did cast some shade on the Pauline writings themselves. Could they be truly orthodox if it was possible for the heretic Marcion to use them to his own purposes?

c) Paul was, again, at the center of theological conflict during the period of Augustine (354-430), a great deal of whose writings were refutations of Pelagianism and its strong insistence on the necessity, or even sufficiency, of human participation in the work of salvation. Augustine's theology was firmly based on the Pauline letters, especially those to the Romans and Galatians. With Paul, he posed the question: "What have you that you did not receive? If then you received it, why do you boast as if it were not a gift?" (1 Cor 4:7).

d) In the 16th century, Paul once more was the personal center around whom the storms of controversy circled. Faith and works, grace and merit, bible and Pope, predestination and free will—battles were fought on many fronts and all with ammunition furnished by the Pauline literature. The controversies of the Reformation period forced all participants to return to the Pauline sources.

e) In our own 20th century, Paul is still a center of Christian discussion, and equally a center of controversy. Women, contesting for complete equality in Christ, can, at one and the same time, utilize Gal 3:28 as their motto and goal, while being justifiably bewildered by a passage such as 1 Cor 14:34-36. Ecumenists, in their difficult endeavors, have at hand an impressive Pauline creed (Eph 4:4-6), plus a powerful theology of the new Adam (1 Cor 15:45-49; Rom 5:12-17), the Body of Christ (1 Cor 6:15-17; 10:16-17; 12:12-13), and faith-baptism as the source of universal personal union with Christ for all Christians (Gal 3:26-27). Students of Church structures research the Pauline churches for signs of an emerging hierarchy (1 Thess 5:12; Phil 1:1; 1 Cor 12:28) and for the even more visible evidence of the gifts of the spirit (1 Cor 12; Rom 5:5; 8:9-10; 12:4-8) bestowed on each of us. And they ask, "How are hierarchy and gifts related?" Finally, for a century in which the Spirit has become once more evident and vital, no books in the Christian scriptures are more important than Paul's. In them the Spirit is a living reality (Rom 8; Gal 5:16-26). Paul is, was, and will be a "man for all seasons," and, often enough, a man to unsettle all seasons.

## 14. PAUL AND THE ACTS OF THE APOSTLES

In this commentary frequent—but critical—use will be made of the Acts of the Apostles as a general background, or historical grid, for the life and letters of Paul. This procedure can be disputed. There are those who characterize *Acts* as a Lukan exercise in imaginative creativity, and refuse to acknowledge its historical usefulness. This author does not belong to that group. The difficulty with Luke is not that he is not an historian but that he is so very much more than that. He wears the caps of many trades. When he wishes to be *an historian* he can be a good one. He prides himself on the research he has done (Lk 1:1-4), affords exact dating for the beginning of the Baptist's ministry (Lk 3:1-2), and—according to experts in the field—is precise both in his political terminology and description of legal procedures. But he is also, and always, *a theologian* whose account of the Emmaus appearance—as one example among hundreds—centers on the eternal question of where Jesus is to be found by today's Christians. In the book, in the bread, in the brethren, says Luke (Lk 24:13-36). He is, moreover, *a preacher* who can combine stories chronologically disparate to form an impressive sermon. The story of Mary and Martha (Lk 10:38-42) has been moved from its proper historical site at Bethany to an unnamed village at the beginning of Jesus' journey to Jerusalem to illustrate what it means to love God. As the Good Samaritan loves neighbor by responding to all his needs, Mary loves God by attentively listening to the words of God's Son. Finally, Luke is also *a literary artist*, enamoured of parallels (annunciations to Zachary and Mary, births of the Baptist and Jesus, beatitudes and woes), and delighted to paint an ascension picture (Acts 1:9-11) utilizing colors taken from the palette of the Elijhan ascension story (2 Kgs 2).

Though Luke is a rich combination of historian, theologian, preacher and literary artist, and must be treated as such, his historical overview has proved serviceable in the laboratory of centuries-long use as a grid for Paul's activities and writings. Note for yourself, as an initial example, how well Luke's account of the Thessalonian apostolate (Acts 17:1-9) and its aftermath (Acts 17:10-18:5) will blend in with the information Paul himself gives in 1 Thess. After all the Lukan criticism of recent years, there is probably only one point in Luke's historical presentation of Paul that causes almost intolerable difficulty. It is the brief remark (Acts 11:30) speaking of a trip by Barnabas and Saul to carry famine relief to Jerusalem. As yet, no one has been able to give a commonly accepted explanation of the difficulty that arises from comparing this one verse with Paul's own account of his visits to Jerusalem in Gal 1:17-2:1.

Luke's Acts, consequently, will be used critically as providing a solid historical picture of Paul's missionary activities. Paul's own descriptions—where they occur—will receive the precedence generally accorded to first-hand testimony.

## 15. OLDEST COPY OF A PAULINE LETTER

No original manuscript of a Pauline letter is in existence today. This is not surprising considering the length of centuries we must back-track to arrive at Paul's period of letter writing in the 50's—and perhaps 60's—of the first century AD. It is even less remarkable when we realize that no original manuscript exists for Shakespeare's plays, all composed in relatively modern times. Yet neither in the case of Paul nor of Shakespeare are we left with serious doubts about the existence and substantial integrity of their writings. Paul was quoted by church writers in the second and third centuries. Even more important, his letters were copied in the original Greek and were translated into all the languages of the Christian commonwealth. The oldest copy of the Pauline literature is found in papyrus 46 (P 46), a codex (book form as opposed to roll) in Greek which can be dated to c. 200 AD. Of this we possess today 86 nearly perfect leaves out of an original of some 104. Originally this codex included ten letters (including the Letter to the Hebrews), all letters to the Churches. It is almost certain that Philemon and the Pastorals (letters to individuals) were not part of the codex. Thirty of the leaves are now in the possession of the University of Michigan at Ann Arbor: the rest are in London. A copy of one of these pages follows. It includes the concluding verses of Philippians, the title to Colossians and the opening verses of that same letter.

## 16. OVERVIEW OF PAULINE LETTERS

The brief resumes which follow attempt to situate Paul's writings chronologically and geographically, and to provide a skeletal review of the letters' contents. Questions about authenticity are mentioned here only in passing.

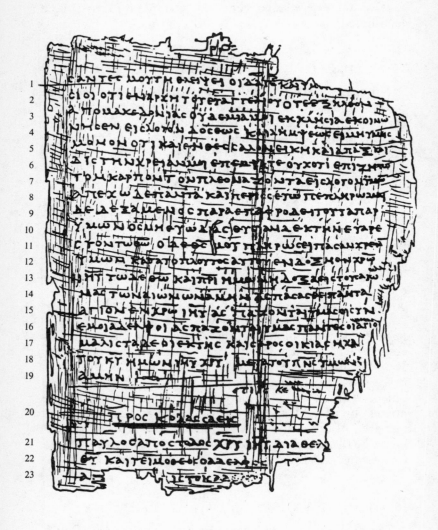

*Oldest copy of a Pauline letter*

**1 THESS**
written c. 51
2nd journey
from Corinth

Probably the first Christian writing which we possess. Partial picture of a Pauline community, mainly Gentile (1:9), some 20 years after Jesus' death. Letter is filled with heartfelt thanksgiving because of the good news which Timothy (3:2-6) has brought. It is also meant as an encouragement under persecution (2:14). Thessalonians "wait for his Son from heaven, whom he raised from the dead" (1:10), and are asked to do so by leading "a life worthy of God" (2:12), a life of sanctification, holiness, love of the brethren (4:1-12). There is *a major stress on parousia,* Christ's second coming (4:13-5:11). Paul expects it during the lifetime of the readers, "we who are alive" (4:15,17). Yet there is no exact timetable. "For you yourselves know well that the day of the Lord will come like a thief in the night" (5:2). Paul asks that the letter be read to the brethren (5:27), presumably in Christian assembly.

---

**2 THESS**
written c. 52
2nd journey
from Corinth

Some questions exist now about the authenticity of 2 Thess after unchallenged acceptance from the time of Marcion's canon c. 140 AD. Yet it is probably best understood as written shortly after 1 Thess—to which it is similar—when Paul received further reports on the parousia difficulty, provoked, seemingly, by a letter purporting to be from Paul (2:2). Treatment of this difficulty forms the heart of 2 Thess (2:1-12). The parousia will not come till after the rebellion and the appearance of the man of lawlessness, the son of perdition (2:3) who is now being restrained by both a *what* and a *who* (2:6-7), all riddles that continue to perplex Pauline interpreters. Letter concludes with a strong statement against idleness. Paul himself lives by his own manual work.

---

**1 COR**
**written c. 56**
**3rd journey**
**from Ephesus**

It followed an earlier letter (5:9), either now lost or forming part of 2 Cor. Paul replies to a myriad of heavy questions, *first from Chloe's people* (factions in 1:10-4:21; incest in 5:1-13; lawsuits in 6:1-11; fornication in 6:12-20) and, *secondly, those contained in a recently received letter from Corinth* (marriage, virginity and widowhood in 7:1-40; idol offerings in 8:1-11; the veil, Eucharist and charisms in 12:1-14:40; the resurrection in 15:1-58). This "problem letter" is filled with Paul's theology: centrality of Christ crucified (1:23); baptism (1:13-17; 6:11; 10:2); Jesus as God's wisdom (1:24, 30), as the Lord of glory (2:8), as the Christian paschal lamb (5:7); Christians as members of Christ (6:15); care not to scandalize the weak (10:23-24); the Eucharist as source of unity (10:16-17) and traditional memorial of Jesus' Last Supper and death (11:23-26); charisms as constructive of Christian community (12:7; 14:3-5, 12, 26); the hymn to charity (c. 13); Christian resurrection as flowing from Jesus' attested resurrection as the New Adam through whom and in whom we, too, shall rise. First mention (16:1-4) of the collection for Jerusalem.

---

**PHIL**
c. 56(?)
3rd journey
from Ephesus

Two problems regarding Philippians: UNITY, is it one letter or an amalgam of several? 4:10-23 could be an individual letter of thanksgiving; 3:2-4:9 could be part of another letter; 1:1-3:1 could indicate still a third letter. Or—think I—the whole is but one letter written over a period of time during which news of the Judaizer crisis forced the obvious break of thought at 3:2. Second problem is LOCALE. Written during captivity (1:7, 13-17) in Rome (attested in Acts), or earlier in Ephesus (a possible deduction from 2 Cor 1:9-10; Acts 19:23-41).
Content = joy in suffering (1:3, 18-19, 25; 3:1; 4:4); unity (2:2-4); the divinity, kenosis and Lordly glorification of Jesus (2:5-11); danger from Judaizers (3:2-11); gospel of righteousness through faith (3:9-11); Paul's special relationship to Philippi (4:14ff).

---

**2 COR**, letters
written over a
period of time
c. 57, partly
from Philippi
(2:13; 7:5)

Refers to a previous severe letter (2:3f; 7:8) which was hardly 1 Cor, and to a second visit to Corinth (2:1; 12:14; 13:1). Seemingly 1 Cor was followed by a severe letter from Paul and his second visit to the city. The present 2 Cor may be a composite of communications with Corinth. Some scholars identify as many as six various communications which have been placed together in editorial unity. Content: Paul's painful letter and visit. Old covenant veiled for those who reject the new (3:12-18). Paul has seen "the glory of God in the face of Christ" (4:5-6). "God was in Christ reconciling the world to himself ...and entrusting to us the message of reconciliation" (5:19). Importance of the collection for Jerusalem (cc. 8-9). Paul's defense of self against the false apostles (cc. 10-13), including his life of suffering as an apostle.

GALATIANS
c. 57
3rd journey
from Philippi ?

An impassioned letter (no thanksgiving) against a non-gospel justification through works of the Law. Biographical details (1:11-2:21). Paul's gospel of justification through faith (2:15-16). Spirit received through faith. Example of Abraham, to whom was made God's unconditioned promise (3:14-18). Law a pedagogue (3:24f). Perfect unity in Christ (3:28). No longer slaves but free children of "Abba, Father" (4:6f). Called to freedom, freedom to love and serve (5:1, 13f). Faith working through love (5:6). Life in the Spirit (5:16-26). Law of Christ (6:2); new creation (6:15), Israel of God (6:16).

ROMANS
c. 58
3rd journey
from Corinth

Mature version of Galatians. Paul's calm and considered presentation of his great themes of sin and justification previous to his hoped-for visits to Jerusalem (15:25), Rome (1:18; 15:24) and Spain (15:24). Power of sin (cc. 1-3). *Abraham's* faith in the life-giving God (c. 4) who, because of love, reconciles humankind (c. 5) in the new Adam through baptismal death and resurrection (c. 6). Law versus Spirit (cc. 7-8). Relationship of Israel and the Gentiles (cc. 9-11). Charisms, charity, government, care of the weak in conscience (cc. 14-15). Paul's travel plans (15:14ff). Recommendation of Phoebe the deaconness (c. 16)—perhaps of independent origin from the rest of the letter.

**COLOSSIANS**
**c. 61**
**captivity in**
**Rome**

Some discussion on authenticity. Epaphras (1:7; 4:12) at Paul's side. Letter written in prison (4:3) to combat aberrant teaching at Colossae, exaggerating the power of angels (2:18) and the necessity of ascetic practices (2:16, 21). Christ presented as HEAD of all creation (2:10), as head, too, of the church (1:18) which is his Body (1:18, 24). Christ's fullness of divinity (2:9). Strong realized eschatology: we are co-buried, co-raised, hidden with Christ in God. Domestic rules of conduct. Tychicus and Onesimus (4:7-9). Luke, the beloved physician (4:14). Letter from Laodicea (4:16)?

**PHILEMON**
**c. 61**
**Roman captivity**

Onesimus (cf. Col 4:9) a slave is returned to Philemon as Paul's child (v. 10), no longer Philemon's slave but as a beloved brother (v. 16). Paul's hope to visit Philemon (v. 22). This letter would have accompanied that to the Colossians.

EPHESIANS    Much dispute about authenticity. A circular letter? Stress on unity and peace. Liturgical. THE MYSTERY = unity of Jew and Gentile in Christ and in Christ with God. Christ, head of Body = Church. Realized eschatology. Ecumenical creed. Moral instructions. Domestic rules of conduct. Tychicus connects this epistle to both Colossians and to Philemon.

## Recommended Readings

Blackman, E.C., *Marcion and His Influence* (London: SPK, 1948). A study of a second-century unorthodox Christian whose advocacy of Paul tended to make the apostle guilty by association.

Bruce, F.F., *Paul: Apostle of the Heart Set Free* (Eerdmans, 1977). An excellent, all-encompassing study of Paul's life, writings, and theology. It has something intelligent to say about every conceivable aspect of Pauline study. The same author speaks of "Paul and the historical Jesus" in the *Bulletin of the John Rylands Library* 56 (1974), 317-35, and provides a resumé regarding research on Acts and the question of its historicity in "The Acts of the Apostles Today" in the same periodical of 1982, 36-56.

Doty, W.G., *Letters in Primitive Christianity* (Fortress, 1973). An excellent resumé of ancient letter writing, with an accent on the early Christian period.

Jewett, R., *A Chronology of Paul's Life* (Fortress, 1979). A profound, but complicated, study of Pauline chronology. It is a challenge even to professional students.

Keck, L., *Paul and His Letters* (Fortress, 1979). A fine introduction to Pauline material.

Krodel, G., *Acts* (Proclamation, 1981). An inexpensive and scholarly treatment of both the content and questioned historicity of Acts.

Martin, R.P., *N.T. Foundations* II (Eerdmans, 1978), 241-247. Treats of "Paul the Letter Writer.'

Mattill, A.J., *Perspectives on Luke-Acts* (Edit. C. Talbert, 1978), 76-98. Gives a balanced presentation of "The Value of Acts as a Source for the Study of Paul."

McHugh, J., *The Mother of Jesus in the New Testament* (Doubleday, 1975) 351-353. Provides a worthwhile description of the difficulties of writing and the use of secretaries at the time of Jesus.

Murphy-O'Connor, J., *Revue Biblique* 89 (1982), 71-91. Deals with one aspect of Pauline chronology in his article, "Pauline Missions Before the Jerusalem Council." Acceptance of his conclusion would necessitate a change in the missionary sequence proposed by Luke's Acts. His *Becoming Human Together* (Glazier, 1982) gives a fine resumé of Paul's theology and anthropology. Pp. 19-32 treat Paul's knowledge of the human Jesus of Nazareth.

Quinn, J., "P[46]—The Pauline Canon," *CBQ* 36 (1974), 379-85. A most interesting article on a codex collection of Paul's epistles toward the end of the second century.

Ricciotti, G., *Paul the Apostle* (Bruce, 1953), 144-147. Has an interesting description of the manner of writing in the 1st century.

Roetzel, C. *The Letters of Paul: Conversations in Context* (Knox, 1975) is another fine introduction to Paul's writings.

Rubenstein, R., *My Brother Paul* (Harper, 1972). A different kind of book on Paul written by a man who is both Jewish and versed in psychoanalytic methodology. His approach is different, and many of his conclusions are unique.

Sherwin-White, A.N., *Roman Society and Roman Law in the New Testament* (Oxford, 1963). A classic study on the legal and administrative accuracy of the Acts and the Synoptic Gospels.

Skeat, T.C., in *The Cambridge History of the Bible* 2 (Cambridge Univ. Press, 1969), 54-79. A fascinating article on "Early Christian Book Production: Papyri and Manuscripts."

Stanley, D., in *Sin, Salvation and the Spirit* (Liturgical Press, 1979), 279-288. Provides an interesting article on the "Significance for Paul of Jesus' Earthly Ministry"

Wiseman, D.J. and Roberts, C.H., in *The Cambridge History of the Bible* 1 (Cambridge Univ. Press, 1970), 30-66. Contains an excellent introduction to "Books in the Ancient World."

# 2

# Paul's First Letter to the Thessalonians

## 1. HISTORICAL BACKGROUND

In all probability, this brief letter was written by Paul from Corinth (Acts 18:1-5) during the second missionary journey and some months after his departure from Thessalonica itself. During this interval he had visited Beroea (Acts 17:10) and Athens (Acts 17:15; 1 Thess 3:1), whence we had sent Timothy to visit the newly-formed Thessalonian Church and to encourage its Christians to bear up under affliction (1 Thess 3:2-6). Timothy's return (with Silas according to Acts 18:5) communicating the good news of their fidelity prompted Paul to write this letter, more than half of which contains some statement of thanksgiving, e.g. 1:2; 2:13; 3:9; 5:18. It is probably *the earliest Christian writing which we possess*, dating to c. 51 AD. It gives us a partial—and precious—glimpse of a young Christian community some 20 years after Jesus' death and resurrection. It enables us to experience the *felt* dedication and loving concern which Paul had for the churches to which his apostolate gave birth.

## 2. IMMEDIATE PREPARATION

It will be helpful to read Acts 17:1-5; 18:1-5 for Luke's description of Paul's ministry in Thessalonica, and for notices concerning the subsequent activities of Paul's Thessalonian adversaries and of Timothy and Silas. Next read 1 Thess at least twice. Here it will prove advantageous to read the text aloud with others, and at a single sitting. Paul's letters were meant to be listened to, and the emotional quality of Paul's language can be felt much more by the ear than by the eye, much more by audition than by reading. Only after this careful reading and listening should you move into a study of the text, utilizing the material which follows.

## 3. 1 THESSALONIANS ACCORDING TO THE CUSTOMARY FORMAT OF PAUL'S LETTERS: INTRODUCTION, THANKSGIVING, BODY, EXHORTATION, CONCLUSION.

### a) *Introduction (1:1)*

Senders = Paul, Silvanus, Timothy (cf. Acts 17:15; 18:5). No title such as apostle or servant is used. Silvanus or Timothy may have served as secretary.

Addressees = Church of the Thessalonians.

Greeting = *grace* (charis), a word used here with multiple significance. It contains the simple idea of "Greetings!" or "Hail!", while, at the same time, intending also the concept of grace as gift, a wish that God gift this audience yet further.

Peace relays the customary Jewish greeting Shalom, with its wish for that wholeness which is integrity in health and in one's relationship with God and neighbor.

### b) *Thanksgiving (1:2-10)*

Paul is especially thankful for the Thessalonians' faith, love and hope (v.3). Insistence on this triad of virtues will eventually culminate in 1 Cor 13, Paul's hymn to love. A second important triad here is God Father, Lord Jesus, and Holy Spirit (vv.3-5). The Thessalonians are encouraged to imitate Paul's own imitation of Jesus in time of affliction (v. 6). They have already become an example in Macedonia (e.g. Philippi), in Achaia (Athens and Corinth) and beyond (v. 8). Paul's statement (v. 9) that these Christians have "turned to God from idols" identifies this congregation as mainly Gentile. He calls upon them to await the return of the risen Jesus (v. 10). It is at this point that Paul introduces in telegram form the central theme of the letter, the return of Jesus. Such an introduction occurs frequently in Paul's thanksgivings.

## c) Body (2:1-3:13)

Contrary to what will become Paul's custom, this section does not stress some dogmatic point but deals, rather, with Paul's personal relationship with the Christian disciples. He recalls the difficulties of his mission (Acts 17:5-9) as well as those at Philippi (v. 2), and, in vv. 3-6, defends himself from what may have been accusations aimed at him by critics. He and his comrades, Silvanus and Timothy, are innocent of error, uncleanness, guile, deception, flattery, greed, pursuit of glory. On the contrary, they have acted both as nursing mothers (v. 7) and as fathers (v. 11) caring for their children while doing manual work for their keep lest they be a burden to the church (v. 9).

Another brief thanksgiving is in order because these Christians accepted the missionaries' preaching "as the word of God, which is at work in you" (v. 13). And they have also accepted the suffering which accompanied the faith.

Vv. 15-16 are sometimes considered a later insertion made sometime after Paul's death and after the destruction of Jerusalem (70 AD) which would be referred to in the phrase "God's wrath" in v. 16. But these verses are found in all copies of this letter and are more probably to be explained as the remark of a Paul frustrated and confused by the strong opposition he has encountered when preaching to the synagogue.

2:17-20 is one of the many passages in 1 Thess revealing Paul's strong love for this congregation. He longs to see these friends again for they are his hope, the evidence of his missionary work when Jesus comes again. It is at this point (v. 19) that the Greek text uses the word *parousia* which means presence, here Jesus' future presence at the time of his return. The word soon became the technical expression for the second coming of Jesus.

3:1-13 consists mainly of personal reflections centered on Timothy, Paul's beloved companion, whom Luke describes as the son of a Jewish mother and Greek father (Acts 16:1). Paul had sent him back to Thessalonica from Athens to encourage the suffering Christians (vv. 1-5) and it is now his return with the good news of their faith and love and courage which has inspired this letter of thanksgiving (vv. 6-13). Paul is absolutely delighted at this good news. He needed it after his own lack of success at Athens (Acts 17) and his immediate difficulties with the mission to Corinth (v. 7, and cf. Act 18).

### d) Exhortation (4:1-5:22)

The fourth section of Paul's customary letter form is clearly evident here. "Finally, brethren, we beseech and *exhort* you in the Lord Jesus..." (4:1). This exhortation concerns three main subjects, chastity, charity, the coming of Jesus, the three "c's" if you wish a memory device.

Chastity (4:3-8): "For this is the will of God, your sanctification; that you abstain from immorality..." (v. 3). Paul spells this out in the male dominated categories of his society, speaking of a man's need to select in Christian fashion a wife (the Greek *skeuos* has a more general meaning than this, but probably does mean wife here in v. 4), and to respect the wife of his neighbor (v. 6). "For God has not called us for uncleanness, but in holiness" (v. 7).

Charity (4:9-12): the text speaks of love for all fellow

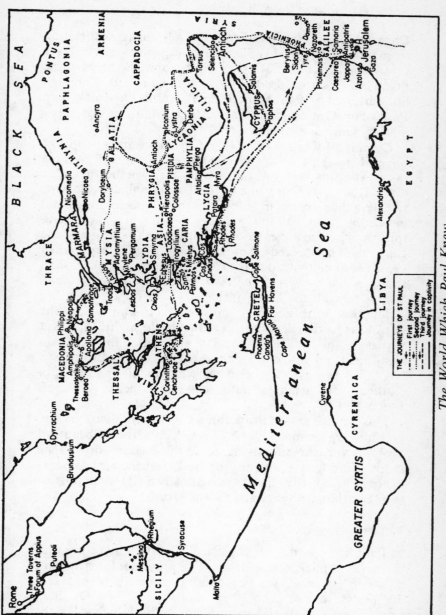

*The World Which Paul Knew.*

Christians (*philadelphia* of v. 9), and adjoins an exhortation
to manual work (v. 11). The encouragement of vv. 11-12
toward civil, prudential living will become the heart of the
much later Pastoral Letters to Timothy and Titus. Though
not authored by Paul himself, the Pastorals have picked up
Paul's constant concern that Christian faith be accompanied by Christian living.

Coming of Christ (4:13-5:11): Christians are a people of
hope. Through Christ and in him, his rising will become
ours. And this is true for all Christians, whether living or
dead. It appears that some of the Thessalonians were worried lest those of their fellow disciples who had died not
benefit by Jesus' coming in glory. Not to worry, says Paul,
for "we who are alive, who are left until the coming of the
Lord, shall not precede those who have fallen asleep." All of
us, those already dead at the time and those still alive, shall
share in the power of the resurrection "and so we shall
always be with the Lord" (4:17).

The time of this coming, however, is unknown for "the
day of the Lord will come like a thief in the night" (5:2). Yet
Christians, as children of the day, children of the light, can
await the Lord with confidence in salvation. The Lord Jesus
has "died for us" (5:10), so we wait for him as disciples
clothed in the armor of faith, love and hope (v. 8, and cf.
Eph 6:13-17).

This set of exhortatory three "c's" is followed by the
multiple suggestions of 5:12-22 which constitute a beautiful
program for Christian living. Read this passage aloud once
more. Note how the trinity of God, Jesus, Spirit appears
again in vv. 18-19. This usage is already a Christian possession less than 20 years after Jesus' death.

### e) Conclusion (5:23-28)

Paul finishes this initial piece of Christian literature with
a brief, but packed, conclusion. He prays confidently that,
at Jesus' coming, we be found completely blameless—
blameless, that is, at the three levels (v. 23) of body (life),
soul (human life), and spirit (human life enriched by the

Spirit). He asks for prayers from all, confident in their efficacy. He sends love, via his messenger carrying the letter, actualized through the Christian kiss of peace (v. 26). He asks, too, that his "letter be read to all the brethren" (v. 27). This suggests that Paul's letters were read at the eucharistic assembly when all the disciples were gathered together. Such a procedure would have been a powerful first step towards eventually viewing them as sacred scripture, on a par with the Jewish scriptures (2 Pet 3:15-16) read in both the temple and during the synagogue worship.

The letter ends as it began: "The grace of our Lord Jesus Christ be with you" (5:28).

## 4. PARTICULAR OBSERVATIONS

a) The *parousia*. This letter was written with the conviction that Jesus would return in the not-distant future (note the "*we* who are still alive" of 4:17), and that it would not be to the disadvantage of those already dead. The Greek word parousia = presence, i.e., Jesus' presence at his second coming, occurs in 2:19; 3:13; 4:15; 5:23, with the most detailed passage being that of 4:13-5:11. The language, especially that of 4:16-17, is highly stylized, and parallels can be found in numerous Old Testament passages where God makes an exceptional appearance on the stage of human history. God's entrance is accompanied by a divine literary fanfare: trumpets sound, earth quakes, mountains heave, and the stage is lit up by flashes of lightning. The language is poetry rather than prose, emotive rather than descriptive. In Paul's own theological and literary development, this type of language became less and less utilized. References in our own century to "the Rapture" (not a biblical expression) derive from 4:17. This turns poetry into prose at the risk of misinterpreting the author. For equivalent God-appearance language in our Jewish scriptures, cf. Ex 19:16-19; Is 27:13; Zeph 1:14-16; Dn 7:13. The earthquake language of Mt 27:50-54; 28:1-4 serves a similar purpose.

b) It has been estimated that 3/5 of this letter is an expression of thanksgiving. This arises from Paul's deep apprecia-

tion of God's goodness to him, and from the intense relief
and pride which he feels at the good news regarding the
Thessalonians' perseverance in faith and in their love for
him (3:6-8). After the lack of success in Athens (Acts 17:16-
34) and the difficulties in the Corinthian ministry (Acts
18:5-7) Paul needs, and now receives and reacts to, human
love and empathy. Timothy's return is like a love letter from
friends.

c) One notes (1:6; 2:14-15; 3:3-4) Paul's conviction that a
dedicated Christian life brings with it a full share in the
sufferings undergone by Jesus who was, indeed, the Christ,
but a servant Christ, a suffering servant Christ. And servant
Christ means servant Christians.

d) This letter introduces us to three Pauline triads, the
first two of which soon become, or are already, common
elements within Christianity: faith, hope and love (1:3; 5:8)
with faith and love in 3:6; God Father, Lord Jesus and Spirit
(1:3-5; 1:6-8; 4:6-8; 5:18-19); spirit, soul and body (5:23).
This final linking occurs only here in the Pauline literature.
Paul alludes in reverse order to the human body, the living
(ensouled) human body, the living body in Christ
(enspirited).

e) Note Paul's extensive use of "brethren - adelphoi,"
taken in its inclusive sense. It can be found 19 times in this
brief letter (1:4; 2:1, 9, 14, 17; 3:2, 7; 4:1, 6, 10 (twice), 13; 5:1,
4, 12, 14, 25, 26, 27). For Paul, *the* Christian relationship is
that of brothers and sisters in Jesus who forms us into the
children of the one parent, God.

f) There are only three uses of the first person singular
(2:18; 3:5; 5:27). Is this a sign that Paul thinks of himself as
writing in close conjunction with Silvanus and Timothy of
1:1?

g) The eight uses of "you know" (1:5; 2:1, 2, 5, 11; 3:3; 4:2;
5:2), plus the "you remember" of 2:9 help to bring Paul's
audience into closer personal relationship. He is speaking
the letter to those to whom it will be read aloud.

h) The letter is filled with Paul's emotional warmth (1:2, 3,
6; 2:7-8; 11-12, 17-19; 3;1-2, 5, 6-13; 5:12-28). These are

friends and beloved Christian brothers and sisters to whom he is writing.

i) Jesus is termed Lord 22 times within this one letter. On five occasions (1:1, 3; 5:9, 24, 28) Paul uses the full phrasing, "Lord Jesus Christ," which constituted the original formal confession of faith for all Christians (Phil 2:11). The human *Jesus* was the *Christ* expected by Judaism, and equally the risen and glorified *Lord* of all humankind.

j) The great Pauline themes are missing, e.g. justification by faith, life in and with Jesus, the Body of Christ, the sacraments. But we do find the first N.T. soteriological statement in 5:10's "who died *for us*." No explanation is given of this terse statement, but Christians have already begun to consider Jesus' death as salvific, as reaching out to them with a divine gift.

# 3

## Paul's Second Letter to the Thessalonians

### 1. HISTORICAL BACKGROUND

This would be the same as for 1 Thess, presuming that 2 Thess followed the former after a brief period of time during which Paul received notice that the gravity of the parousia problem was weightier than he had previously imagined. A letter purporting to be from Paul (2 Thess 2:2) may have increased the agitation. Talking of historical background, of course, presumes the authenticity of this letter, a disputed question which will be confronted only after the reader has become better acquainted with the letter's content.

### 2. IMMEDIATE PREPARATION

Here, again, you are asked to read—or listen to—this brief letter at least twice in a small group setting. What did you hear that struck your attention?

# 3. CONTENT ACCORDING TO CUSTOMARY LITERARY FORMAT

## a) Introduction (1:1-2)

This is almost identical to that of 1 Thess. Same senders, same addressees, same greeting, but with the addition of v. 2's "from God the Father and the Lord Jesus Christ." Cf. similar greetings in Rom 1:7; 1 Cor. 1:3; 2 Cor 1:2; Gal 1:3; Eph 1:2; Phil 1:2; Col 1:2; Phm 1:3. This is Paul's salutation.

## b) Thanksgiving (1:3-12)

Paul is grateful for the Thessalonians' faith, love, and perseverance in trial (vv. 3-4).

There follows a description of the parousia, presented in apocalyptic language (v.7), and sharply divisive into two world groups. There are, on the one hand, those who know not God (the Gentiles) and those who do not obey the gospel of Jesus (unbelievers to whom the gospel has been preached), and, on the other, the saints who have believed (vv. 8-10). The language here, as in 1 Thess 2:13-16, is in sharp black and white contrasts, similar to passages in Ps 79:5-6 and Jer 10:25. This strong polarity is early Paul, still growing in his knowledge of God's incredible goodness to all humankind. In Romans 2:6-16, a later and more mature letter, Paul recognizes with gratitude the loving God's open door policy to all.

The prayer of vv. 11-12 brings the chapter to a peaceful conclusion, but not before the theme of the letter, the parousia, has been presented. Paul's thanksgivings, as already mentioned, usually contain a subtle introduction to the theme(s) of the letter.

## c) Body (2:1-17)

The heart of this letter is its insistence that the day of the Lord has yet to come (v. 2), but that it will definitely come. Paul gives no exact timetable, but, like the evangelists who will follow him (Mk 13; Mt 24; Lk 21), he is willing to provide a rough calendar. Before the Lord's coming, there must first occur "the rebellion—*apostasia*" and the appearance of the man of lawlessness, the son of perdition, who takes his seat in the very sanctuary of the temple, proclaiming himself to be God (vv. 3-4). At the moment, however, this demonic (v. 9) movement is being restrained by both a "what" (v. 6) and a "he" (v. 7). This short section of 2:3-7 is the proverbial secret wrapped up in a secret. "Do you not remember that when I was still with you, I told you this? And you know. . . " (vv. 5-6). Again, one side of a dialogue! Presumably the Thessalonians know and remember, but, unfortunately, we do not. It is clear that the text intends to defuse the anxious concerns which are multiplying with regard to Jesus' coming. The specifics, however, can only be guessed at. One expects an extensive religious rebellion, the apostasia of v. 3, (and cf. Mt 24:10-13), led by an individual, "the man of lawlessness, the son of perdition," who, in blasphemous pride, pretends to divinity. This is an antichrist figure such as will be mentioned specifically in 1 Jn 2:18, 22; 4:3; 2 Jn 7. His features, not surprisingly, are drawn from historical characters who have menaced God's people in recent, and very recent, history. Both Antiochus IV of Syria and Gaius Caligula come to mind. Antiochus, in 167 BC, placed the altar of the Greek god Zeus over the Jewish altar of holocausts in the temple (the abomination of desolation spoken of in Dn 8:13), thus provoking the successful uprising of the Maccabees. Caligula, the mad Roman emperor, ordered a colossal statue of himself to be set up in the temple c. 40 AD, barely ten years before 2 Thess was written. Caligula was unsuccessful in his attempt, but the terrible threat lingered on in memory.

What is unclear is the meaning of vv. 6-7. Restraining this mystery of lawlessness is both a *what* (v. 6) and a *he* (v. 7). Who and what are holding back the satanic (v. 9) movement?

One fairly popular explanation is that which interprets the Roman empire as the *what*, and the emperor as the *who*. Preventing the spread of lawlessness would be the peace-providing power of Rome. A second explanation moves in an entirely different direction. *What* restrains the ultimate outbreak of evil is the necessity that the gospel be promulgated throughout the world (Rom 11:25; Mk 13:10; Mt 24:14f.; Lk 21:24) and *he who* is at the center of this missionary work is Paul himself. Neither explanation has received common approval of scholars, and the problem is still with us.

A second thanksgiving follows in 2:13-17. It begins as did the first, "We are bound to give thanks to God always for you, brethren" (2:13; 1:3), and centers its thanks on God's choice of these disciples, on God's love for them, on their sanctification and call to glory. Thoughts of God, Lord and Spirit fill the passage. Paul's reference to traditions taught to the Thessalonians either orally or by *letter* probably alludes to 1 Thess. This short section concludes with the comforting prayer of vv. 16-17. God's gift is love, comfort, hope and firmness; the Christian response must be an integration of work and word (v. 17).

### d) Exhortation (3:1-15)

With a "Finally, brethren" (3:1), Paul turns to a series of exhortations. He asks for prayer (cf. 1 Thess 5:25) so that the Lord's word may prosper and that he be unhindered in his work (vv. 1-2). He prays, too, for these new Christians that they be strengthened to live confidently in accord with God's love and Christ's faithfulness. This is followed by a strong exhortation against idleness (vv. 6-15). Paul himself is proposed as an example. He ate his bread at the sweat of his own brow and wishes all who are capable of work to do the same. Both by temperament and by religious conviction, Paul has difficulty with a picture of Christians "living in idleness, mere busybodies, not doing any work" (v. 11). He hopes that such persons will be embarrassed by opposing Christian reaction, yet not as though they were enemies but as brothers and sisters of the same family (v. 15).

### e) Conclusion (3:16-18)

Paul prays with repeated determination that God's *peace*

be with them *all* at *all* times in *all* ways. He adds to the letter—written by a secretary?—his own personal signature to verify its origin from him (cf. 1 Cor 16:21; Gal 6:11). And he concludes with a final blessing (v. 18).

## 4. OBSERVATIONS

a) Reminding us of 1 Thess is this further insistence on "brothers—adelphoi," here nine times in the three chapters (1:3; 2:1, 13, 15; 3:1, 6 (twice), 13, 15) as well as the triads of Lord, God, Spirit (2:13) and of faith/love in 1:3 together with love/hope in 2:16. There is, moreover, a literary similarity between

| | | |
|---|---|---|
| 2 Thess 1:1-2a | and | 1 Thess 1:1; |
| 2 Thess 1:3 | and | 1 Thess 1:2-3; |
| 2 Thess 1:5 | and | 1 Thess 2:12; |
| 2 Thess 2:16-17 | and | 1 Thess 3:11-13; |
| 2 Thess 3:8 | and | 1 Thess 2:9; |
| 2 Thess 3:18 | and | 1 Thess 5:28. |

b) The authenticity of this letter is the final point for consideration. After 18 centuries of unchallenged acceptance - cited as Paul's by Polycarp (Phil 11:4) early in the 2nd century and included in Marcion's canon (c. 140 AD) -the letter's authenticity was first challenged at the beginning of the 19th century. Criticism centers on 2 Thess 2:1-12 which, according to some scholars, is irreconcilable with 1 Thess 4:13-5:11.

Thus, 1 Thess 5:1's "But as to the times and seasons, brethren, you have no need to have anything written to you" could be judged contradictory to 2 Thess where it becomes obvious that further instruction of the Thessalonians was necessary.

Again, 1 Thess 5:2 says that "the day of the Lord will come like a thief in the night" whereas 2:3ff gives an apocalyptic timetable of Jesus' coming.

Personally, I'm not impressed by the preceding arguments. Regarding the first, Paul could have underestimated the parousia difficulty in his first letter and returned to it in his second when later reports from Thessalonica demanded further explanation. Besides, the phrasing "you have no need to have anything written to you" is a Pauline statement of confidence, a personal appeal which does not at all preclude further instruction. Just a few verses earlier (in 1 Thess 4:9) Paul assures the Thessalonians that they "have no need to have anyone write" them concerning love of the brethren, yet he does so himself in the following verses.

Regarding the second difficulty, an apocalyptic warning need not consider suddenness as contradictory to a timetable. The same mixture is found in Mk 13:6-10 (preparatory signs) and 13:33-37 (unexpected arrival).

A final argument sometimes used against authenticity is that the vocabulary and style of the two letters are so similar that the second must have been written by a Pauline copyist. This, surely, is part of a "Catch 22" situation. If the vocabulary and style were completely different, then the authors would be different, too: if they are very similar, then the authors can't be the same. It makes more sense to say that the similarities of 1-2 Thess are those to be expected in letters written by the same author to the same people under similar circumstances regarding a similar problem and within a brief period of time. "All in all it seems preferable to conclude that 2 Thess was written by the author of 1 Thess, who was probably Paul but may have been Silvanus or Timothy; if so, it must have been written about the time of 1 Thess because of the similarity of language and structure" E. Best, *The First and Second Epistles to the Thessalonians* (1972), 58. Disbelievers in the authenticity of 2 Thess must still provide a rationale for its production. What purpose can it have served? Why would it have been written?

## Recommended Readings

Best, E., *A commentary on the First and Second Epistles to the Thessalonians* (Harper & Row, 1972). This may well be the best commentary in English on these two letters. It is scholarly, well-written, with a use of the original Greek which is not prohibitive for the ordinary reader. Best argues that 2 Thess is an authentic letter of Paul, though he may have used either Silvanus or Timothy (1 Thess 1:1; 2 Thess 1:1) as his secretary.

P. Ellis has given us a useful commentary in *Seven Pauline Letters* (Liturgical Press, 1982). He does not, however, treat 2 Thess since its authenticity is disputed. He is extremely optimistic about finding an A-B-A pattern in all of Paul's writings, but he does give us much help in understanding Paul's message.

I. Havener has produced a popular pamphlet commentary on *1 Thessalonians, Philippians, Philemon, 2 Thessalonians Colossians, Ephesians* (Liturgical Press: CBC #8, 1983). This includes brief introductions to, and commentaries on, 1-2 Thessalonians. Aimed at an ordinary reading public, it may mystify and confuse its readers by treating 1 Thess 2:13-16 as an appendix, a later addition to the original letter. Though this is a possibility, it is hardly the certainty that Havener claims. He has separated the treatment of the Letters to the Thessalonians since he is convinced that Paul did not author the second volume.

J. Reese, *1 and 2 Thessalonians* (M. Glazier: NT Message #16, 1979). This is another popular commentary of decent length and depth. Paul is the author of 2 Thess. "Those who argue for its non-Pauline origin have not provided satisfactory motive for its existence" (xv).

# 4

# Paul's First Letter
# to the Corinthians

## 1. HISTORICAL BACKGROUND

Paul had evangelized Corinth during his second mission-ary journey (Acts 18:1-18), after his experiences in Philippi, Thessalonica, Beroea, and Athens. The encounter with Gal-lio (Acts 18:12ff) allows us to date Paul's stay in Corinth with unaccustomed accuracy. Gallio was proconsul in Corinth 51-52 AD. Paul remained in Corinth c. two years (Acts 18:11, 18), helped by Silas and Timothy (Acts 18:5), as well as by Aquila and Priscilla, recently arrived from Rome (Acts 18:2-3). Their combined apostolate seems to have been particularly successful among the synagogue Greeks (Acts 18:4) such as Titus Justus (Acts 18:7), Gentile "God-fearers" who, though unwilling to accept circumcision and the Mosaic law, frequented the synagogue because of the attraction of its monotheism, ethical principles and prayer life.

Corinth was both a metropolis on the isthmus connecting the N-S land masses of Macedonia and Achaia, and a notable meeting place of E-W cultures due to its double seaports. About five miles to its east lay the port of Cench-reae opening out to the East. Two and a half miles to the north was the sister port of Lechaeum opening out to the West and to Rome. Corinth's population, consequently, was very much a mixed bag of nationalities from the Medi-

terranean basin and from the Near East. All populations
and all social classes rubbed shoulders together in this bus-
tling city. Paul's letter was occasioned by the humanly
understandable rise of a whole multitude of problems in this
young church. These problems were relayed to Paul in
person by "Chloe's people" (1:11), and indirectly by means
of a letter (7:1) which may have been carried to Paul by
Stephanas, Fortunatus and Achaicus (16:17). Paul's
response in 1 Cor was written in Ephesus (1 Cor 16:8, 19) c.
56-57 AD.

## 2. IMMEDIATE PREPARATION

Read, first, the Lukan account in Acts 18. Follow this
with an initial reading of 1 Cor, and then by a second
reading utilizing the skeleton outline provided on p. 67. The
outline will help to keep the issues distinct and easy to
commit to memory. Further readings can utilize the literary
format schema which follows, as well as the presentation of
problems and solutions found on pp. 68-83.

## 3. 1 CORINTHIANS ACCORDING TO PAUL'S LITERARY FORMAT

### a) Introduction (1:1-3):

Sender—Paul and Sosthenes (secretary?). There is a certain emphasis on Paul's authority, "called by the will of God
to be an apostle of Jesus Christ," which is not found in 1-2
Thess.

Addressees—the church of God in Corinth, together with
all Christians.

Greeting—grace and peace.

### b) Thanksgiving (1:4-9):

Thanksgiving manages to introduce the subjects (important within this letter) of spiritual enrichment, gifted speech
and knowledge, spiritual gifts, perseverance and Christian
fellowship.

## c) Body (1:10-15:58):

I—Chloe's people (1:10-6:20)
II—The Letter (7:1-15:58)

### PART I—Report from Chloe's People (1:10-6:20)

i—Problem of factions (1:10-4:21) advocating personal centers such as Paul, or Apollos (1:12; 3:4-6, 22; 4:6; 16:12; Acts 18:24-19:1), or Cephas or Christ. Apollos we know from Acts 18:24-19:1. Was his approach more scholarly than Paul's? Cephas? Had he visited Corinth (1 Cor 9:5), or does this refer to Christians of a strong Jewish bent? And Christ? Perhaps this indicates charismatic enthusiasts who claimed the Spirit of Jesus as their source of knowledge and action.

Paul is bothered throughout this section by an appeal to wisdom on the part of at least some of the Corinthians. Wisdom, too, is what Paul advocates, but a different wisdom, the wisdom manifest in what appears to be the supreme scandal and foolishness of the crucified Christ. In Christ crucified are found the wisdom and the power of God (1:24, 30). Paul summons all factions to common unity in him who was crucified for us and in whom we have been baptized (1:13), in him who is indeed "the Lord of glory" (2:8), sharing the name and nature of Yahweh (Ps 24:7-10; Acts 7:2). Paul's extensive reference to wisdom—"sophia = wisdom" is used 15 times from 1:21-3:19—must intend to refute an "elite" among the Corinthian Christians who considered themselves especially privileged and enriched in their knowledge of the faith.

ii—The problem of incest (5:1-13). A man is living with "his father's wife," hardly his mother, but probably a step-mother. To the previous arrogance of knowledge is added the arrogance of action. Paul judges the person's accepted presence in the community as a corrupting leaven to be cast out—"that his spirit may be saved" (5:5)—from the presence of "Christ, our paschal lamb" (5:7), just as leaven would be removed from a Jewish house during the passover feast. A Christian of Paul's church was expected to present the image of Christ to the world. How else could the world recognize the presence of the Lord?

iii—The Problem of Lawsuits between Christians (6:1-11). Certainly lawsuits between Christians before unbelievers (6:6) are just the opposite of what Paul wills. Can't such sad affairs be handled by fellow Christians (6:5)? Or avoided completely by Christian tolerance and forgiveness (6:7, and cf. Mt 5:39-42)? Paul's appeal to an avoidance of sin is based on baptism in which they were "washed...sanctified...justified in the name of the Lord Jesus Christ and in the Spirit of our God" (6:11). In the Pauline churches of the 50's, therefore, baptism could be explained as a sanctifying, justifying *washing* effected by the Lord and the Spirit of God. We are already close to the complete Trinitarian formula of Mt 28:19.

iv—The problem of fornication (6:12-20). Further arrogance of action! "All things are lawful" is a working rule for some Corinthians who apply it also to sexual conduct. To this rule—perhaps drawn from Paul's insistence on the Gentiles' freedom from the Law—has been added a justifying argument. Just as food is meant for the stomach and the stomach for food, so intercourse is meant for the body and the body for intercourse. Paul will have none of this; he refuses the parallelism. Food and stomach are temporary, limited to this world. The body is not; it is meant for the Lord. Corinthian Christians are given a choice: union with Christ or union with a prostitute. Our bodies are the members of Christ. The language is strong, it is also corporal. Union with the woman's body or union with the risen, glorified body of the Lord? Which will they choose? "So glorify God in your body," says Paul (6:20).

PART II—Response to the Letter (7:1-15:58)

i—Marriage, Virginity, Widows (7:1-40), a difficult NT section.

*Marriage* (vv. 1-24). Paul insists that marriage is legitimate (vv. 2, 9) and that it presumes a basic equality between husband and wife (vv. 2-5). Motivation for marriage does not include here the personal values advanced by the twentieth century, nor even the "sacramental" presentation of Eph 5:21-23, i.e. marriage as a sign of the union between Christ and the Church.

Paul insists, secondly, that marriage is indissoluble (vv. 10-11), and for this teaching he has the word of the Lord to fall back on (Mk 10:2-12; Mt 5:31-32; 19:3-9; Lk 16:18). Paul wants to keep marriage alive and together. Yet in the case of a Christian married to an unbeliever, he appreciates the possible destruction of peace and permits the disruption of the marriage (vv. 12-16). In general, Paul has developed a personal principle of the "status quo". Better to remain as God called us—married or unmarried, circumcised or not, slave or free (vv. 17-24). Paul himself is unmarried (never married? a widower?), and he sees advantages to that (vv. 7-8).

*Virginity* (vv. 25-38). In fact, all things considered, Paul would vote in favor of virginity when feasible. And this because of impending disaster, in preparation for which one should be concentrating on the Lord (vv. 25-31). It is easy to be reminded here of Jeremiah's celibacy as a sign of the imminent fall of Jerusalem (Jer 16:1-4). A further reason for celibacy is Paul's hope and expectation—not always verified—that dedicated celibacy can make for "undivided devotion to the Lord" (v. 35). Certainly, in Paul's own case, it provided him with exceptional personal freedom for his missionary apostolate. But marriage itself, insists the apostle, "is no sin" (v. 36).

*Widows* (vv. 39-40), says Paul in conclusion, can marry in the Lord, but perhaps are better off to remain as they are.

Paul walks a narrow tightrope throughout this chapter, indicating a clear preference that people remain in the state in which they were called (vv. 8, 17, 20, 24, 26, 40), while, at the same time, granting his readers a complete freedom of choice (vv. 6-7, 9, 15, 21, 35-39).

ii—Idol Offerings (8:1-11:1)

Frequently food for sale in the markets had been offered to the gods. Did this vitiate its use for Christians?

There is a strong initial preference for love over knowledge (8:1-11). Again we encounter the supposed Christian elite. Yet "knowledge puffs up, but love builds up" (8:1). Love will prevent our justified freedom from becoming a stumbling block to the weak (8:9) for whom Christ died (8:11). So, too, Paul will subordinate his freedom to the good of others, in particular his right to material support. Though an apostle, one who has actually seen the Lord Jesus (9:1), he suspends his own rights. He becomes all things to all people, bending himself to them (9:1-23). Paul runs in the hope of winning, and with the necessary effort (9:24-27). So should the Corinthians (10:13) to whom is given the ominous example of Israelite failure in the desert, interpreted through Christian categories of baptism, eucharist, and the new Moses (10:1-4).

And now back to the point, food offered to idols.

—Shun idol worship, a communication with demons who stand behind the idols even though the images and food sacrificed to them are of no value.

—Make your choice, what will it be: pagan sacrifices and union with demons? Israel's sacrifices and union in the altar? or participation in the body and blood of Christ? "Because the bread is one, we the many are one body, for we all partake of the one bread" (10:17).

The final answer—so long in coming—to the idol food difficulty depends not on whether something is lawful, but whether or not it builds up the community (10:23-24). Therefore:

—eat what is sold in the market place, and without scruple;

—eat what is served at a friend's house;

—avoid scandalizing the weak. "So, whether you eat or drink, or whatever you do, do all to the glory of God" (10:31).

iii—Problems Regarding Proper Order at Christian Worship (11:2-14:40).

*Woman's Veil* (11:2-16). This is an odd little section, timely rather than timeless. It is not even agreed that the argument concerns a woman's veil—the terminology is ambiguous—though that is still the common opinion. And if, indeed, a woman's veil is at the center of the discussion, why? There is some evidence that only prostitutes went without a veil in Paul's world. Certainly, parts of the Jewish world—like Philo's contemporary Alexandria—kept women hidden as much as possible. Paul responds with various arguments, a sign, surely, that he was not completely satisfied with any of them.

—Argument from Scripture: God is head (origin?) of Christ who is head of man who is head of woman. The veil in some way indicates this order which Paul finds in Gen 2:18. Yet man is dependent for birth on woman (v. 12).

—Argument from nature (vv. 13-15). It is only natural that men wear their hair short and women long.

Finally, the sociological argument from common practice: "...we recognize no other practice, nor do the churches of God" (v. 16).

*Eucharist and The Common Meal, The Agape* (11:17-34). This involves a breakdown of brother- and sisterhood at the precise moment when it should have been felt and demonstrated most acutely. Paul is justifiably irate. "Shall I commend you in this? No, I will not" (v. 22).

This is the first written description of the Last Supper and it is given in words already ritualized and handed down to Paul (vv. 23-26). Evidently this gives us the central text of the eucharistic worship in Paul's churches. It points in two directions: to the eucharist as representative of the Last Supper (v. 23), and to the eucharist as memorial to Jesus' death (v. 26). Paul is not surprised that even physical evils beset those who eat and drink without discernment (vv. 29-30). V. 34's "About the other things..." reminds us, once more, of the missing half of the dialogue.

Charisms (12:1-14:40). The picture given here, perhaps one-sided because of the necessity to handle problems which have risen, is that of a highly charismatic church easily prey to the dangers of uncontrolled enthusiasm. Paul calls it back to the essentials.

—There is one basic creed, "Jesus is Lord," in direct opposition to the belief that Jesus, because of his crucifixion (Dt 21:22-23) had been cursed (12:3).

—Gifts have but one origin, the Spirit-Lord-God of 12:4-6, 11, as they have but one purpose, the common good (12:7). Each Christian shares in these gifts, just as all corporal members share in the one body. This is the way it is with Christ (12:12), the risen Lord into whose glorified body we have all been joined by baptism and by drinking of the Spirit in Eucharist (12:13). Paul, throughout 12:4-30, is emphasizing the truth, so clear to him, that the gifts should build up the body, should unite, and not be a cause of disunion and prideful disrespect. He mentions some of the gifted people: those especially gifted in wisdom, or knowledge, or faith, the healers and miracle workers, prophets, discerners, speakers in tongues and their interpreters (12:8-10). All are gifted by the Spirit (12:11), and all need each other's gifts (12:14-26). A second, more institutional list of gifted persons follows: apostles, prophets, teachers, miracle workers, healers, helpers, administrators, speakers in tongues (12:28-30).

—But, if you want to be REALLY GIFTED, love is the answer (13:1-13). Although this ode to love can stand in beautiful independence and may have had an origin anterior to this letter, it is also true that the virtues proposed in vv. 4-7 and the repeated treatment of tongues, prophecy and knowledge render it particularly apt for the Corinthian situation. They constitute a strong argument in favor of its Pauline composition precisely at this time and for this occasion.

—The final chapter on charism (14:1-40) insists on one point, that the gifts should be used to upbuild (root meaning of *edify*) the Church. Paul returns to this theme again and again (vv. 3, 4, 5, 12, 17-18, 26). Clear prophetic instruction, consequently, is thousands of times more valuable than speaking in tongues (v. 19). Is the reference, again, to the Corinthian elite?

—Paul finally presents the procedure to follow (vv. 27-31). Two or three speakers in tongues, if someone can interpret. Two or three prophetic utterances. And, for God's sake, let's have peace (v. 33).

—Vv. 33b-36 stun us with their seemingly blunt and

unexpected content. Is Paul putting down the women? Or is it the Corinthian men, whose opinion would be expressed in vv. 34-35, whom he is chastising? Surely it is remarkable that v. 36 speaks to the *men*—"...are you the only ones" in the masculine gender—where one would expect a final reference to the women.

iv—The Resurrection (14:1-58).

Is there a resurrection? Is it even conceivable, or possible, that future life is at all related to this *physical me* whom the Greeks regarded as personal prison of the soul? Sōma (body) = sēma (tomb) was their conception; the body was a tomb from which the soul escaped, finally and eternally, at death.

Paul first testifies to the FACTS, to the known witnesses, including himself. The language is solemn: "I delivered to you as of first importance what I also received" (15:3). The long list of witnesses follows. He next argues from a theological principle. Because of union with Christ, his resurrection and ours are two sides of the same coin (vv. 12-19). Subtract the one and you destroy the other. But, as a matter of fact, Jesus has risen and is now the new Adam (v. 22) in whom we will all be made to live. To these arguments of historical witness and theological principle, Paul adds two arguments of lesser persuasion, the usage by some of baptism for the dead (v. 29)—a practice whose procedure and purpose elude us—and Paul's own willingness to suffer all, to virtually die, out of his resurrection belief (vv. 30-32).

So much for the fact of resurrection. Regarding the manner—What will it be like?—Paul is reduced to analogy (vv. 35-43). It will be somewhat like the metamorphosis of a seed which descends into the ground, only to rise to a transformed existence. We, too, shall be transformed in the new Adam (vv. 45-49). The glorified Christ whom Paul has actually seen (1 Cor 9:1; 15:8) is the heavenly being whose image we shall become (v. 49).

d) *Exhortation (16:1-18).*

This letter has been long, filled with Corinthian problems and Paul's attempts to help. So now this exhortation can be brief. A *collection* is being made "for the saints" in Jerusalem. Contribute at the assembly "on the first day of every week" (16:2). Journeys are to be made. Paul will be going to Macedonia (Philippi, surely) and Corinth, but will remain on in Ephesus until Pentecost (vv. 5-9). Timothy should arrive in Corinth, but Apollos will not be going—at least not for the moment (vv. 10-12). Mention is made of Stephanas, Fortunatus and Achaicus who, perhaps, carried the letter of 7:1 together with personal explanations of the situation in Corinth. They seem to be church officials of some kind, since the Corinthians are exhorted "to be subject to such men" (v. 16).

*e) Conclusion (16:19-24)*

Greetings from the "churches of Asia," from Aquila and Prisca and the members of their house church (Acts 18:19, 26), together with all the Christians of Ephesus (vv. 19-20). Reference to the "holy kiss" (v. 20) may well indicate that Paul intends this letter to be read in the eucharistic assembly.

Paul greets his audience by adding a few words in his own hand.

"Marana Tha" (v. 22) means "Lord, come," a prayer expressed here in the original Aramaic of the earliest Church rather than in Paul's Greek.

There are final greetings of grace and love (vv. 23-24).

## 4. A SKELETON OUTLINE OF 1 CORINTHIANS

This is provided with the hope that it will be a second, and more visual, way of becoming acquainted with 1 Corinthians. Memorizing the order of this letter will make more personal and more stable both its content and the order of its unfolding.

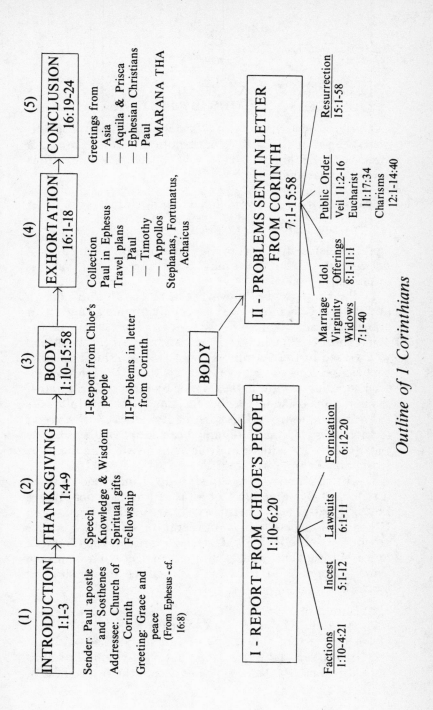

| (1) | (2) | (3) | (4) | (5) |
|---|---|---|---|---|
| INTRODUCTION 1:1-3 | THANKSGIVING 1:4-9 | BODY 1:10-15:58 | EXHORTATION 16:1-18 | CONCLUSION 16:19-24 |

**INTRODUCTION 1:1-3**

Sender: Paul apostle and Sosthenes
Addressee: Church of Corinth
Greeting: Grace and peace
(From Ephesus - cf. 16:8)

**THANKSGIVING 1:4-9**

Speech
Knowledge & Wisdom
Spiritual gifts
Fellowship

**BODY 1:10-15:58**

I-Report from Chloe's people
II-Problems in letter from Corinth

**EXHORTATION 16:1-18**

Collection
Paul in Ephesus
Travel plans
 — Paul
 — Timothy
 — Appollos
Stephanas, Fortunatus, Achaicus

**CONCLUSION 16:19-24**

Greetings from
 — Asia
 — Aquila & Prisca
 — Ephesian Christians
 — Paul
      MARANA THA

**BODY**

**I - REPORT FROM CHLOE'S PEOPLE 1:10-6:20**

Factions 1:10-4:21
Incest 5:1-12
Lawsuits 6:1-11
Fornication 6:12-20

**II - PROBLEMS SENT IN LETTER FROM CORINTH 7:1-15:58**

Marriage Virginity Widows 7:1-40
Idol Offerings 8:1-11:1
Public Order
  Veil 11:2-16
  Eucharist 11:17:34
  Charisms 12:1-14:40
Resurrection 15:1-58

*Outline of 1 Corinthians*

## 5. 1 CORINTHIANS ACCORDING TO ITS PROBLEMS, SOLUTIONS, BY-PRODUCTS

This is a third viewing of this rich text. What problems have been sent to Paul? What solutions does he provide? Are there theological "by-products" that Paul mentions simply in passing?

*I. Report from Chloe's People* (1:10-6:20)

(1) Factions (1:10-4:21)

a) Problems: division among Christians following lines of *personalities* who also may have represented various interests.

i—Paul: at least we know what he had to do with Corinth and what his theology was, especially after reading 1 Cor and Romans.

ii—Apollos: "...a native of Alexandria...an eloquent man well versed in the Scriptures" (Acts 18:24). Eloquence and biblical exegesis must have been his forte. Was he considered superior to Paul in these fields by certain Corinthians?

iii—Cephas: had he ever been to Corinth so that followers formed a clique around his personality? Does 1 Cor 9:5 refer to such a visit? Or has he simply been adopted as symbol by those Christians still strongly Jewish, insistent on the Law, feasts and Temple worship?

iv—Christ: and what is this group? Connected in some way to Jesus' relatives (1 Cor 9:5)? Or, more probably, are these Spirit-gifted Christians, charismatics, for whom Christ's Spirit is the only consideration, and who consider as inferior those less gifted? "They represent the slogan of hyper-spiritual enthusiasts who see no need for any human leader." So A.C. THISELTON, "Realized Eschatology at Corinth," *NTS* 24 (1978), 514.

b) Solution:
i—Basic union in the one Christ through baptism.
ii—Basic essential doctrine of Christ crucified—folly to the Greeks, scandal to the Jews, but *wisdom and power* to the Christians. Paul's is a plea to accept the foolishness of

God rather than the supposed wisdom of men.

> God's plan was not wise (1:17-25).
> God's subjects are not wise (1:26-31).
> Paul's preaching was not in wisdom (2:1-5).

iii—The apostles are simply servants (3:5), fellow-workmen for God (3:9), servants of Christ and stewards of the mysteries of God (4:1). Yet Paul is also the Corinthians' father in Christ Jesus through the Gospel (4:15).

c) Theological by-products

i—Jesus is "the Lord of glory" (2:8). This is high Christology, predicating of Jesus the divine terminology found in Ps 24:7-10.

ii—The presentation of Jesus as the wisdom of God (1:24, 30) is part of a wide movement in early theology that evidences itself not only in Paul but also in Matthew/Luke and John. Both Matt 11:25-30 and Lk 10:21-22 present Jesus as God's wisdom, meant to reveal God to the little ones. In even more insistent fashion, the Fourth Gospel revolves completely around the concept of Jesus as the incarnate revealer of who and what God is. Through the Son, the Father bespeaks himself. The Son is, consequently, God's *word*, the divine *logos*.

iii—The Corinthians are God's temple, indwelt by God's Spirit (3:16f).

(2) Incest (5:1-13)

a) Problem: a man living with his father's wife. This is not the culprit's mother, but his step-mother. His father may be already dead, or perhaps has divorced the woman. But marriage within that relationship was forbidden by Lev 18:8; 20:11 and condemned also by the Gentiles. (Cf. BARRETT, First Epistle to the Corinthians, p. 121 who quotes both Cicero and Gaius to that effect.)

b) Solution: the man is to be banished from the group, excommunicated, handed over "to Satan for the destruction of the flesh, that his spirit may be saved in the day of the Lord Jesus" (5:5). Paul hopes that the offender may recognize the seriousness of the sin from the gravity of the punishment, and seek reconciliation. Paul wants very much that this young Christian community be a model of Christian living to the non-believing world.

c) Theological by-products

i—"For Christ, our paschal lamb, has been sacrificed" (5:7). The language is a strong statement (a Pauline original? already traditional?) of the centrality and efficacy of Jesus' death in Christian theology c. 56 A.D. There is a new passover victim, a new passover salvation, a new passover feast.

ii—Some in Corinth are boasting about this type of free sexual behavior (5:2, 6). There appears to be a feeling among some that their new existence in the Spirit has freed them from serious consideration of the body. For the "spiritual," what one does with one's body is inconsequential. This becomes a strand in the thinking of Gnostic circles of the second century AD.

iii—5:9 speaks of a previous letter written by Paul to Corinth. It is either completely lost, or—according to some scholars—is partially contained in II Corinthians.

(3) Lawsuits (6:1-11)

a) Problem: Christians are bringing other Christians before the civil magistrates. This, for Paul, is not only washing community laundry in public, but proof positive that there is such laundry to wash.

b) Solution: "Why not rather suffer wrong? Why not rather be defrauded?" (6:7). Or, if that is demanding too high a level of Christian sufferance, there must be someone "among you wise enough to decide between members" of the community (6:5).

c) Theological by-products: "But you were *washed*, you were *sanctified*, you were *justified* in the *name* of the Lord *Jesus Christ* and in the *Spirit* of our *God*" (6:11). The reference is certainly to Christian baptism and to the sanctification and justification which are its companions. Baptism is theologized as a *washing*, the most evident sign-meaning of the sacrament, but Paul's theology of baptism will have much more extensive development in Romans 6. The conclusion of the verse is hardly a baptismal formula, yet its mention of *Jesus* the *Spirit*, *God* brings it close to the actual formula of Mt 28:19.

## (4) Fornication (6:12-20)

a) Problem: Some Christians, acting upon what seems to be a Corinthian Christian slogan, "All things are lawful for me" (v. 12), a slogan that could easily have come from Paul himself but in a different context, are claiming that fornication is permissible. The mentality here seems similar to that seen in the case of incest: for the spiritual, what is done to or with bodies is beneath consideration or scruple. Besides, intercourse—they say—is as natural for the body as food for the stomach. "Since no corporal action has any importance, everything is permitted" Murphy-O'Connor, "Christian Slogans in 1 Cor 6:12-20," CBQ 40 (July 1978), 396.

b) Solution: Not at all! The body has become "a temple of the Holy Spirit within you...So, glorify God in your body" (6:19-20). Choose either spiritual union with Christ's body or carnal union with that of the prostitute (vv. 15-17). The latter union destroys the former. Intercourse is not to the body as food to the stomach, a necessary product. Food, stomach, intercourse are all temporal realities. The body, on the contrary, is meant for eternity, "not meant for immorality, but for the Lord and the Lord for the body" (6:13).

c) Theological by-product: In the center of his argument Paul presents—and for the first time in Christian literature—his doctrine on the Body of Christ. *The language, in my opinion, is strongly corporal.* The case offers two options: carnal union with the woman's body ("one body with her", v. 16), or union (in one spirit) with the present, risen, glorified body of Christ. This latter union is just as real, personal and intimate as the former. Only the manner of union is different. In union with Christ's glorified body

we become his members (v. 15) and achieve a type of identification with him, plus a strong union with each other,
fellow-members of the same body.

## II. *Responses to the letter (7:1-15:58)*

### (5) Marriage, Virginity, Widowhood (7:1-40)

This chapter is one of the most difficult to exegete in the
N.T. Here, clearly, it would be so helpful to know what the
Corinthians had written in their letter. Our ignorance on
this point makes clarity difficult, as does the Greek of some
of the individual verses.

#### *Marriage* (vv. 1-24)

a) Problem(s): Our first verse is a problem in itself. What
is the function of "It is well for a man not to touch a woman"
(7:1), and whose opinion does this represent? Is this a Pauline emphasis, or is this a slogan made by some of the
Corinthians to which Paul is reacting? If the former, Paul is
counselling against marriage; if the latter, Paul is counselling ascetic, celibate-minded Christians (some of whom are
already married) to be less forceful and more prudent in
their stance.

b) Solution: I believe that the latter is Paul's position.
Denying that marriage is sinful (v. 28), he reminds the
Corinthians of some of the facts of life: that celibacy has
temptations of its own (vv. 2, 8-9); that husband and wife
belong equally to each other (vv. 2-5); that prolonged absti-
nence in marriage can also be a temptation (v. 5); that
divorce has been forbidden by the Lord (vv. 10-11); that a
previous marriage between a new Christian convert and a
pagan spouse should be kept alive if possible (vv. 12-16).

c) By-products:
i—Paul introduces into the discussion a strong statement
in favor of remaining in the "status quo" (vv. 17-24). Persuaded that the time till the parousia is short (vv. 29, 31),
and that it will be filled with difficulty (v. 26), he believes it
more prudent to remain as one is, concentrating on *undivided devotion to the Lord* (v. 35).

ii—As Paul speaks of marriage, his balanced presentation of male and female rights is surprising for those times. Vv. 2-5 are a clear example of this. The same is true in vv. 10-11. The wife should not separate from her husband, just as the husband should not divorce his wife.

iii—Vv. 7-8 tell us that Paul is unmarried as he writes, and that he intends to remain so. Has he been a lifelong celibate, contrary to the ordinary rhythm of Jewish life, or is he a widower? Lack of evidence allows no definite answer here.

## *Virginity* (vv. 25-38)

a) Problem: What about the unmarried? Should they remain that way?

b) Solutions: Paul has no word from the Lord here (v. 25), but personally he favors virginity for two reasons.

i—Because of the distress during the final days (v. 26). One is reminded of Jeremiah, counselled by God to remain celibate because of the disastrous times which were to accompany the destruction of Jerusalem (Jer 16:1-4).

ii—To secure "undivided devotion to the Lord" (v. 35). This personal solution, however, is not at all a command (vv. 25, 28 , 35). The Corinthian Christians remain free to marry, and in some instances positively should (vv. 8-9). This discussion introduces the case mentioned in vv. 36-38. It is here that the Greek text is ambiguous. Does it speak of a father and his marriageable daughter? Of a young man and his fiancée, deciding whether or not to go ahead into marriage? Of two young people who had determined on a type of Christian brother-sister love?

## *Widows* (vv. 39-40)

Here, at least and at last, the issue is clear. Marriage is dissolved by the death of one of the partners. A widow then becomes free to marry again, though Paul believes she would be happier, more blessed (same adjective as in the beatitudes) to remain unmarried. Yet, if this is not her gift, marriage is advisable (vv. 8-9).

## (6) Idol Offerings (8:1-11:1)

a) The Problem: Corinth, an international city situated between two nearby seaports, was rife with pagan cults, an amalgam of Greco-Roman deities cross-fertilized by Oriental religions. The numerous guilds, too, had their deities and religious rites. A large share of the meat offerings was not consumed in the actual services but found its way into the public market. What should be the Christian position regarding the purchase and consumption of such meat? And would Christians be allowed—as workers and as citizens— to attend pagan rites (marriages, funerals, guild services, thanksgivings) since they believed that pagan gods were non-entities?

b) Solutions: Paul wends his way through two-and-a-half chapters before giving his practical solution in very brief and ordered form.

i—The good of one's neighbor must be the primary consideration (10:22-24, 28).

ii—Eat whatever is sold in the market place without scruple (10:25).

iii—Accept a supper invitation from a non-Christian with no difficulty and eat what is set before you (10:27-28).

iv—Avoid eating food which has been offered in sacrifice if this offends the weak conscience of another Christian (10:28).

v—Avoid pagan services of idol worship (10:14). The idol, indeed, is nothing, nor is food offered to it intrinsically changed, but demons and demonic powers do exist. A Christian cannot have it both ways: shall we share in sacrifices to pagan gods, or in the body and blood of Christ (10:16-21)?

c) By-products:

i—Paul's main ethical principle is that in Christ we are children of God, brothers and sisters one to another, called to act as such. This includes, in a special way, care of the weak. Our knowledge may easily puff us up, but it is love that builds—us individually and the community (8:1-3). Paul will avoid, consequently, whatever scandalizes a fellow Christian (8:7-13; 10:28-29).

ii—Chapters eight through ten demonstrate Paul's capacity and penchant to follow a type of psychological sequence. He stays right on the subject of idol offerings in c. 8; moves from curtailment of freedom in 8:9-13 to the various rights he has given up as an apostle to eliminate putting any "obstacle in the way of the gospel of Christ" (9:1-23); concludes with an appeal to caution lest any of us be overconfident as were our Jewish ancestors in the desert (9:24-10:13). It is only after this serpentine trek that Paul comes up with the precise solution.

iii—"Have I not seen Jesus our Lord"(9:1)? Paul has seen the Lord and this vision now controls the whole of his Christian life. Jesus is not the cursed criminal of Dt 21:22-23 whose followers Saul persecuted, but the exalted Lord of Is 52:13-53:12.

iv—Almost in passing, Paul offers us some invaluable material on the sacraments. 10:1-3 speak of Moses and the Exodus from a Christian point of view. (Paul could never have written this as Saul the Jew.) The Christian analogue to 10:1-3 is that Christians pass through the water to be baptized into Christ, and that all Christians eat the same supernatural food and drink the same supernatural drink. This is a clear, though indirect, reference to baptism and the Eucharist.

v—10:14-22 is another clear reference to the Eucharist as a participation in the blood and in the body of Christ. Furthermore, this participating unites us to one another. Because there is just one bread (the body of Christ in 11:24) we, though many, become one body because we all eat of the one loaf (which is Christ's body). I am speaking here as one who believes in the presence of Christ in the Eucharist and who believes that Christ's eucharistic body—which is his risen and glorified body—unites all Christians into Christ's Body (with a capital B) which in Colossians and Ephesians will be called the Church. I do not view the expression "Body of Christ," indicating Christ and his members, as basically metaphor. We are Christ's Body because in faith-

/ baptism and through the Eucharist we are united to Christ's risen body, now become "life-giving spirit" (1 Cor 15:45).

vi—10:23 repeats the "All things are lawful" slogan of 6:12. Paul is being beaten again with his own club. What he expressed as freedom from the law was now being used to argue to freedom from moral principles. Paul definitely has moral principles.

## (7) Public Order (11:2-14:40).

What we find here is a series of three problems all concerned with the Christian assemblies.

### The Veil (11:2-16)

a) The problem here that obfuscates the text is not so much the "one-half of a dialogue" letter characteristic as the sociology of the period. Is it that Paul's pro-veil mentality rises from the Corinthian scene where not to wear the veil marked a woman as a prostitute? Or does Paul start from a heavily Jewish background in which the society kept Jewish women at home, deep in the recesses of the house, and veiled when on the street (cf. J. Jeremias, *Jerusalem in the Time of Jesus,* 359-376)? Or, as some recent authors suggest, does the problem concern men with long hair looking like women, and women with cut hair looking like men?

b) Solution: Paul takes three tries at an answer. His *first* is theological. Appealing to the order of the Genesis creation story (Gn 2:18ff), Paul sees God-Adam-Eve. To this he can, and must, add Christ, and the formation becomes God-Christ-Adam-Eve. God is head and source of Christ, Christ is head and source of Adam, Adam is head and source of Eve. Woman's veil in some way indicates this order of precedence. Yet Paul hesitates: "Nevertheless, in the Lord woman is not independent of man nor man of woman; for as woman was made from man, so man is now born of woman" (11:11f).

Paul must not have been completely satisfied with this

logic, since he moves to a second consideration, one from the law of nature. A woman's long hair is her pride, but a man's long hair is degrading. (Cf. a parallel from Epictetus in Barrett, *First Epistle to the Corinthians,* 256f.)

Paul is running out of arguments. His final one, a sociological solution to a sociological problem, is simple: "...we recognize no other practice, nor do the churches of God" (v. 16).

c) By-product: V. 5 gives us an unexpected view into a Christian assembly in the 50's where women are both praying and prophesying in public. Paul does not argue against the fact (and this will jar against 14:34f), but centers in on the manner. They should be veiled when praying and prophesying in the assembly, yet their active participation is presumed.

## The Eucharist (11:17-34)

a) The problem: the first Eucharist was observed in the midst of a supper. The Eucharist at Corinth followed similar lines, only that the more leisurely rich had both time and provisions to do things up right (and wrong), while the poor had less time and less food and drink. Some started to eat before others, some drank too much, some went hungry. Paul was infuriated.

b) The solution: "So then, my brethren, when you come together to eat, wait for one another—if anyone is hungry, let him eat at home—lest you come together to be condemned" (vv. 33-34). The Eucharist is a Christian celebration of thanksgiving, of shared fellowship in the Lord, a memorial of Christ's death. It's neither free lunch at a neighborhood bar, nor a New Year's Eve party.

c) By-products:

i—In reaction to the Christian abuses at Corinth, Paul has given us the first literary description of Christian Eucharist and of the Last Supper. His description in vv. 24-25 resembles closely the text of institution in Lk 22:19-20.

Presumably Paul is using a text which was in liturgical use in his own churches and may well have been derived from Antioch.

ii—V. 25 stresses the *new covenant*, the fulfillment of the centuries-old promise of Jeremiah 31:31.

iii—The Eucharist is intimately related, not only to the Last Supper, but to Jesus' crucifixion. "For as often as you eat this bread and drink the cup, you proclaim the Lord's death until he comes" (v. 26).

iv—Paul expects that an unworthy reception of bread and cup will bring its own punishment, even corporal. (Cf. similar thought concerning incest in 5:5.) In Paul's world, divine and demonic powers are both close to hand.

v—V. 34 is a fine example of the 1/2 dialogue, "about the other things I will give directions when I come." What other things?

## *Charisms* (12:1-14:40)

a) Problem: Corinth was a Church singularly rich in gifts of the Spirit: the utterance of wisdom and of knowledge, faith, healing, miracles, prophecy, distinguishing of spirits, tongues, interpretation of tongues (12:8-10). But this plethora of gifts was turning into a source of confusion. The gift of tongues, especially, was causing difficulty. It was breaking spontaneously into the worship service, at times in choral form as more than one person took over simultaneously. Great confusion! And even when only one person spoke in tongues, what was the advantage? Who drew good from it?

b) Solution: Paul wants worship to proceed peacefully and in order so that *all may be truly built up* (edified). Each has a contribution, surely: a hymn, a lesson, a revelation, a tongue, an interpretation. Let those with the gift of tongues proceed in order, two or three at the most, but only if someone can interpret. Let the prophets speak so that all may learn and be encouraged (14:26-31), for the prophets speak clearly to all "for their upbuilding and encouragement and consolation...he who prophesies edifies the church" (14:3-4).

c) By-products:

i—Just in passing, Paul has contributed to Christian centuries one of the most moving hymns ever penned, the hymn to charity in c. 13. It need not be his own creation, he may have learned it elsewhere, but its appropriateness for the Corinthian problems argues in favor of its creation precisely on this occasion. It is presented simply to stress the fact that the gift of all gifts is love—greater than faith, greater than hope, greater than the extraordinary spiritual charisms of which the Corinthians were so proud.

ii—A fair amount of Body of Christ material also appears. Compressed into 12:12-13 is its whole theology. As the human body is one with many members, *so is Christ*. (Note, not so is the Church, or so are you, but so is Christ.) "By one Spirit we were all *baptized* into one body (Christ's)—Jews or Greeks, slaves or free—and all were made to *drink* of one Spirit" (12:13). With this, Paul centers on Jesus' body into which all, irrespective of race or rank, are united *through baptism and Eucharist*. This is again, not a metaphor. But, the concrete reality established, Paul can then use metaphorical language (like a body) which he does in 12:14ff. Not only are we members of Christ's risen body, but as such we can be likened to a human body with its unity and diversity. And so we get the ear, eye, nose, hand, head and feet of 12:16-21. But Paul's thinking does not start with metaphor; that is an afterthought. We can note in v. 21 that Paul does not yet think of Christ as head of the Body (this terminology will occur in Colossians and Ephesians), though 11:3 may be his first step in that direction.

iii—Paul gives a loose ordering of functions and gifts in 12:28: "first apostles, second prophets, third teachers, then workers of miracles, then healers, helpers, administrators, speakers in various kinds of tongues." This listing of apostles, prophets and teachers as being of primary importance tends to tie the charisms to institutional functions. Later centuries exaggerated this to the point of *limiting* the charisms to institutional officials.

iv—One of the most difficult problems in this section on charisms is the brief passage of 14:33b-36. On the face of it, Paul, quite simply and rudely, limits women to passive presence in the church assembly. They are gifted with the charism of silence! What are the possible explanations of this difficult passage?

(A) Provoked by the letter's (7:1) presentation of disorderly assemblies in Corinth, Paul is reacting strongly to a feminist movement within the Corinthian Church. In this case, some women in Corinth were moving fast and hard for the equality idealized in Gal 3:28 and symbolized in the equal-sex sacrament of Christian baptism. From what Paul hears, they are moving too fast and causing dissension and resentment in the community. This is one opinion.

(B) These verses are a later interpolation in Paul's text effected by someone who shared the opinion of 1 Tim 2:11-12, "Let a woman learn in silence with all submissiveness. I permit no woman to teach or to have authority over men; she is to keep silent." Arguing in favor of such an interpolation theory are:

-1- 14:33b-36 seems to contradict the picture of women praying and prophesying in church which Paul has already presented with approval in 11:5.

-2- There exists some textual difficulty. Vv. 34-35 are found elsewhere, i.e. after 14:40, the end of the chapter, in some manuscripts. This suggests that they may have originated as a marginal note, later incorporated into the text at different places.

-3- V. 34 sounds un-Pauline. "...they should be subordinate as the law says." It is stunning to find Paul arguing toward behavior determined by the law, Paul for whom "the power of sin is the law" (15:56).

For these reasons an increasing number of scholars (e.g. C.H. Barrett, F. Cleary, H. Conzelmann, L. Cope, R. Fuller, D. Georgi, L. Keck, J. Murphy-O'Connor, C. Roetzel) are convinced that we have here an interpolation which betrays the equal status doctrine of Paul evidenced directly in Gal 3:28 and indirectly in his lavish praise of women co-workers in Rom 16:1-15. Did they co-work in silence? Did Priscilla teach Apollos by hand signals? (Acts 18:26)

(C) Recently Edwina Hunter and Neal Flanagan (BTB, 11, Jan 1981, 10-12) have proposed the theory that vv. 34-35 are, in fact, a quotation from the letter of 7:1 expressing the opinion of *the men* whom Paul chides in v. 36. In this case, the negative content of vv. 34-35 would not be Paul's opinion but a statement directly contrary to his personal thought. In favor of this theory are the following points.

-1- First Corinthians is replete with verses which various commentators have identified as statements quoted from various Corinthian groups. Thus, e.g.

| | |
|---|---|
| (1:12) | "I belong to Paul...I belong to Apollos...I belong to Cephas...I belong to Christ." |
| (2:15) | "The spiritual man judges all things, but is himself to be judged by no one." |
| (6:12; 10:23) | "All things are lawful." |
| (6:13) | "Food is meant for the stomach and the stomach for food." |
| (7:1) | "It is well for a man not to touch a woman." |
| (8:1) | "All of us possess knowledge." |
| (8:4) | "An idol has no real existence...there is no God but one." |
| (8:8) | "Food will not commend us to God. We are no worse off if we do not eat, and no better off if we do." |
| (11:2) | seems to be Paul's indirect quotation of a Corinthian statement which read, "We remember you in everything and maintain the traditions even as you have delivered them to us." |
| (15:12) | "There is no resurrection of the dead." |

-2- It is *possible*, therefore, that Paul is quoting from the Corinthians in vv. 34-35. What argues to *the fact* that he is so doing?

a) V. 36 is truly puzzling when read in the original Greek or in a very precise translation. The RSV reads: "What! Did the word of God originate with you, or are you the *only ones* it has reached?" Strangely, the *"only ones—monous"* is masculine. Paul is now talking to the men where we would expect just the opposite. Vv. 34-35 concern the women. Why, then, does v. 36 chide the men? All this would make sense if, or only if, vv. 34-35 are a quote from a men's group of Jewish Christians to which Paul responds with some indignation in v. 36. The text, with the addition of one explanatory parenthesis would thus read: "The women (you say) should keep silence in the churches. For they are not permitted to speak, but should be subordinate, as even the law says. If there is anything they desire to know, let them ask their husbands at home. For it is shameful for a woman to speak in Church." Thus far the men. Paul's answer (v. 36) would then follow in opposition. "What! Did the word of God originate with you, or are *you men the only ones* it has reached?" Paul would then conclude the whole treatment with vv. 37-40.

b) This theory puts Paul in agreement with his treatment of women in both 1 Cor 11:5 and Gal 3:28. The Paul who will preach equality in Gal 3:28 and who already allows women to pray and prophesy in 1 Cor 11:5 would be the same Paul who contests male dominance in 1 Cor 14:36.

c) With this explanation, the argument from law would not be Paul's but his opponents'. And, indeed, it doesn't fit Paul.

## (8) Resurrection (15:1-58)

a) Problem: As if Paul had not already faced enough problems in this extraordinary letter, one more major one remains. *What of Christian resurrection?* The precise nuance here can go in one of two directions, or perhaps in both at once. Is it that some Corinthians were denying future resurrection because they believed that they had already risen with Christ, as evidenced in the gifts? This would be a gnostic-like, spiritually elite stance. Or does the difficulty rise from the Greek philosophy of sōma = sēma, i.e. that the body is a tomb in which the soul is encased until its liberation at death? I believe that Paul's argumentation is directed against the latter position.

b) Solution: There will be future resurrection for Christians quite simply because Christ rose and was seen by definite witnesses. What has happened to Christ will, because of our union with him, happen to us. Christ's resurrection and ours are two sides of the same coin: if the resurrection of Christ is a fact--and the witnesses are named to substantiate it—then our resurrection, too, is guaranteed.

c) By-products:

i—For Paul, the resurrection of Christ is the central, primary and indispensable doctrine of Christianity. Not only is Jesus the risen Lord, but *God is the God who raised Jesus from the dead*: "...if Christ has not been raised, then our preaching is in vain and your faith is in vain" (v. 14).

ii—Using a formula already fixed in tradition, "I delivered to you...what I also received" (v. 3, and cf. 11:23 for the Eucharist) Paul lists the witnesses to the resurrection, many of whom are still living: Cephas, the Twelve, the more than 500, James. And, lastly, Paul himself (and cf. 1 Cor 9:1).

iii—Regarding the manner of the resurrection, Paul must work from analogy. As the seed rises in changed form, so shall our seeded bodies rise imperishable, glorified, in power, and spiritual (vv. 36f, 42-44). We shall be like what Christ has become; we shall be transformed by the life-giving Spirit of the last Adam (v. 45). With this (and v. 22) Paul has introduced the second Adam theology which will prove important in Romans 5.

## 6. CONCLUSIONS

a) This long letter which we have approached from three different avenues is deep in problems—some quite time-bound—and extraordinarily rich in timeless theology. Paul, for the first time in extant Christian literature, speaks to us of Jesus as the "power of God and the wisdom of God" (1:24), as "the Lord of glory" (2:8), as "our paschal lamb (which) has been sacrificed" (6:7). Christians have become, individually, "a temple of the Holy Spirit" (6:19). They are, moreover, "members of Christ...united to the Lord" (6:15, 17), "baptized into one body...and all...made to drink of the one Spirit" (12:13). Partaking of the one loaf, they "who are many are one body" (10:17). This eucharist which unites us into the risen body of Christ—we are what we eat—is also a moving memorial of Jesus' last supper (11:23), as well as a solemn proclamation of "the death of the Lord until he comes" (11:26). Strange to say, Paul's eucharistic theology appears only in 1 Corinthians, so we must be grateful—in ironic fashion—for the Corinthian sinners who gave rise to these Pauline statements. There is also an exhilarating theology of the gifts possessed by all Christians whereby they join together to build up the Church. And we are also presented with an extraordinary emphasis on the resurrection of both Jesus and all Christians. The actual witnesses to the resurrection are named and numbered, and we are reminded that Jesus' metamorphosis in the state of glory is the model and the guarantee of our own.

b) The reader of 1 Cor can hardly avoid a final judgment of admiration for the creative theology of Paul. Presented with what seems to be an endless list of problems, with no library to refer to except his Jewish scriptures, with no moral theologians or academic journals to consult, Paul has moulded his responses out of his own emerging understanding of Jesus, man and risen Lord. He is the first Christian theologian of whom we have written record. After twenty centuries of further theologizing, Paul remains, undoubtedly, the first Christian theologian and, in all probability, the best.

## Recommended Readings

Barrett, C.K., *The First Epistle to the Corinthians* (Harper & Row, 1968) remains an excellent commentary. It makes wise use of the Greek text without confusing non-academic students. It provides a detailed analysis of each section, preceded by an adequate introduction.

Ellis, P., *Seven Pauline Letters* (Liturgical Press, 1982), 38-114. An up-to-date commentary on this letter.

Getty, M.A., has authored *First Corinthians-Second Corinthians* as #8 in the Collegeville Bible Commentaries, 1983. It presents a fine exegesis, plus introduction, plus photos, a Pauline map and study questions.

Meeks, W.A., *The First Urban Christians* (Yale Univ. Press, 1983). Builds on the fact that Pauline Christianity was entirely urban. Meeks, consequently, studies the urban background of Paul's churches, unearthing in the process valuable information about the church in Corinth.

J. Murphy-O'Connor has written extensively on Paul's relationship to Corinth. His *St. Paul's Corinth* (Glazier: Good News Studies #6, 1983) is a fascinating study of the classical texts speaking of the city. Some are tied directly to Paul's era. Archaeology is enlisted to clarify the situation of the house churches of the community.

The same author has provided an excellent, and sometimes challenging commentary on *1 Corinthians* (N.T. Message, #10, 1979). He has also written an article, "Sex and Logic in 1 Corinthians 11:2-16," *CBQ* 42 (1980), 482-500 which challenges the customary interpretation of the "women's veil" problem.

A.C. Thistleton has given students of Paul an invaluable introduction to the Corinthian literature in "Realized Eschatology at Corinth," *NTS* 24 (1978), 510-526. He believes that most of the problems in that community were provoked by elitists whose exaggerated attitudes were shattering church unity.

*The Bible Today*, Vol 18, #6 (Nov 1980) has a series of four articles dealing with 1 Cor. Aimed at ordinary readers, it gives an overview of the letter, followed by individual articles on christology, and on the Spirit and unity in the Body of Christ.

# 5

## Paul's Second Letter to the Corinthians

### 1. LITERARY BACKGROUND

a) In treating the preceding letters (1-2 Thess, 1 Cor) it was possible to speak of the probable time and place of composition. In the case of 2 Cor, however, the situation is much more complicated. The major preliminary question regarding 2 Cor concerns its unity, or lack thereof. The letter, as we now have it, contains major shifts in topics, sharply different emotions, repetitions, paragraphs that don't fit into context. Because of this, the majority of commentators—but not all—see in 2 Cor a composite letter, a selection of Paul's genuine writings that have been combined by an unknown editor into one synthesized letter. Exactly how many writings have been combined is not agreed upon. Some authors believe there were only two original letters, the present chapters 1-9 and 10-13. Others propose three, cc. 1-8, c. 9, cc. 10-13. Others suggest four, adding to the preceding list a supposed Pauline note found in 6:14-7:1. My own opinion is that we find in 2 Cor a combination of six different Pauline writings which we will label with letters (A) through (F). Briefly presented, they are the following.

(A) 1:1-2:13 plus 7:5-16. This is a *letter of comfort*, a letter in which Paul expresses his deep consolation at the resolution of his problems with the Corinthian community, problems which are expressed in anguished fashion in cc. 10-13.

This letter of comfort is calm and happy, filled with personal recollections. The later section enclosed in 7:5-16 seems to be part of this letter, too, since 2:13 is followed naturally by 7:5 and the "comforts" of cc. 1-2 are paralleled by those of 7:6-13. The comfort Paul found in Titus (7:6-7) stemmed from the positive effect caused by Paul's previous and painful letter mentioned in 7:8, 12; 2:4. Seemingly, the conflict with Corinth has now been successfully resolved.

(B) 2:14-7:4 is a beautiful piece of writing in which Paul, while defending his ministry, emphasizes confidence, the new covenant and the new creation, and the reconciliation which God has effected for us in Christ. The tone of these chapters indicates a less difficult period before Paul's emergency visit (2:1) and the painful letter (2:4; 7:8).

(C) Within this section, however, 6:14-7:1 treat of what looks like an unrelated subject. Note how 6:14ff break the tone of 6:11-13 which is more naturally followed by 7:2. The content of this section is similar to that of Paul's lost letter mentioned in 1 Cor 5:9-13. It also has striking parallels in thought to that of documents from Qumran's Dead Sea Scrolls.

(D) 8:1-24 may have been, originally, a short letter of recommendation for Titus as he moved into Corinth to follow the progress of the monetary collection for the Church at Jerusalem.

(E) 9:1-15 appears to have been, at one time, independent from c. 8, though the two chapters share much common material. It concerns the collection, not only in Corinth but throughout the churches of Achaia.

(F) 10:1-13:14 may be the main part of the "painful letter" mentioned in 2:4 and 7:8. Paul feels constrained to present his own qualifications as Christ's minister in response to the contrary claims of "super-apostles" (11:5; 12:1). The letter speaks in 12:14; 13:1-2 of Paul's plans for a *third visit* to Corinth and its boisterous Christians. This postulates between Paul's founding stay in Corinth (Acts 18) and the hoped-for third visit (cf. Acts 20:1-2 for an allusion to this visit during which *Romans* was written) both Paul's second visit and this "painful letter." Section (A) described above would be the consoling end of the dispute, a reconciliation between Paul and whatever adversaries he had in the Corinthian Church.

One scholarly proposal is that this varied material was joined together into 2 Cor toward the end of the 1st century when, as we know from the letter called *I Clement*, the Corinthian Church was again threatened by contentious disunity. The editor of 2 Cor might have judged his finished work as quite parallel in literary structure to the customary letters of Paul along the following lines:

Introduction and Blessing/ Thanksgiving (1:1-11)
Body: (1)  Paul's defense of his ministry (1:12-7:16)
      (2)  Christian charity collection for the Jerusalem Church (cc. 8-9)
      (3)  Paul's spirited apologia for his apostleship (cc. 10-13:10)
Conclusion: Final appeals, greetings and blessings (13:11-13)

b) Tentative ordering of Paul's Corinthian correspondence

| Chronological Order | Description of the Pauline writing |
| --- | --- |
| -1- | Lost letter of 1 Cor 5:9-13. "I wrote to you in my letter not to associate with immoral persons..." |
| -2- | Our present 1 Corinthians |
| | *Pieces of six letters proposed for 2 Corinthians* |

-5-    (A) 1:1-2:13 plus 7:5-16 = Letter of comfort and reconciliation. It reads as though the unsettling conflict between Paul and elements of the Corinthian Church has been successfully and happily resolved.

-3-    (B) 2:14-7:4 = a letter of mild defense before Paul's emergency visit to Corinth and a following painful letter. Within this section appears

-1?-    (C) 6:14-7:1 = a bit of the lost letter of 1 Cor 5:9-13 preserved here in 2 Cor?

-6?-    (D) 8:1-24 = a *collection* letter to Corinth, recommending Titus together with the brother famous in all the churches for the preaching of the gospel (v. 18), plus another brother mentioned in v. 22.

-7?-    (E) 9:1-15 = another *collection* letter in which Paul sends along the brethren (v. 3), but with no mention of Titus. The addressees may include more churches in Achaia (v. 2) than those of Corinth.

-4-    (F) 10:1-13:14 = a core part of Paul's painful letter to Corinth mentioned in 2 Cor 2:4; 7:8.

This is all a bit confusing, no doubt, but a slow reading of the text with a personal effort to follow the division suggested will make this complicated presentation more comprehensible. It is, as has been noted, tentative. I make my own the sage comment of the following exegete: "No one who has made a serious attempt to study the Corinthian situation is likely to feel convinced that he has a monopoly of truth" (C.K. Barrett, *The Second Epistle to the Corinthians,* 1973, p. 6).

## 2. COMMENTS ON THE CONTENT OF 2 CORINTHIANS

(A) 1:1—2:13; 7:5—16. Presumably this is a letter (part of a letter?) of reconciliation after the terrible dispute with the Corinthians has been resolved. Paul identifies himself as Jesus' apostle because that fact is so important in his relationship with the Corinthians. Timothy is with Paul at this time. He is missing from the introduction to 1 Cor since he was already on the road to Corinth when 1 Cor was composed (1 Cor 4:17; 16:10-11).

The blessing (1:3-11) substitutes for the ordinary Pauline thanksgiving (missing only here and in Galatians) to which it is thematically related. Its heavy accent is on "comfort" (ten times in vv. 3-7 alone), a feeling which must have overwhelmed Paul at the resolution of his major fallout with the Corinthian Christians. Christian suffering leads to Christian comfort.

Vv. 8-10, which speak of Paul's extreme difficulties in Asia, constitute a foundation for the widespread belief that Paul's turbulent stay in Ephesus (Acts 19:23-40) included a spell in prison from which, *perhaps*, two of the captivity letters (Philippians and Philemon) were composed.

V. 9's "God who raises the dead" gives us a casual assertion of the very center of Paul's theology.

In vv. 15-22 the difficulty with Paul's travel plans is complicated.

(1) In 1 Cor 16:5 Paul intends to go to Macedonia and then to Corinth.

(2) 2 Cor 1:16 has Paul going first to Corinth, then to Macedonia, with a hoped-for return to Corinth, and then on to Judea (Jerusalem).

(3) Seemingly, changed plan (1) for half of plan (2), i.e. he went straight to Corinth (the second and difficult visit), then on to Macedonia, but without returning to Corinth. This third visit will be planned in 12:14 and 13:1. It is this changing of plans that enables some of Paul's adversaries to accuse him of vacillation and indecisiveness. But, says Paul, so far as the gospel message is concerned, his response is a constant "Yes," just as Jesus, himself, is the yes-fulfillment of God's promises.

1:23-2:13. Paul eliminated the proposed return trip to Corinth because it would have been too painful, "another painful visit" (2:1). But he encourages all involved to pardon any troublemaker in Corinth, "to reaffirm their love for him" (2:8). Him will Paul, too, pardon.

After Paul had left Ephesus, he journeyed to Troas, hoping to find Titus there with good news regarding Corinth.

Disappointed at Titus' absence, Paul moved on to Macedonia (Philippi).

7:5-16 is the logical conclusion to this section. Paul, in deep discomfort, was overjoyed at the arrival of Titus with the good news "of your longing, your mourning, your zeal for me" (v. 7). At last, after 1 Cor, after the painful visit followed by the letter of tears, the pieces are coming into place. Paul's soul is at peace. The painful letter (cc. 10-13) accomplished its purpose by effecting "godly grief" (vv. 9, 10, 11). The "comfort" of which Paul spoke in 1:3-7 is now balanced (inclusion) by the "comfort" expressed in 7:6-7, 13.

(B) 2:14-7:4. In general, this is a calm defense of Paul's ministry, written probably before the painful visit and the succeeding letter. (In its present position it includes with it letter (C), the brief section from 6:4-7:1). Paul's defense is an unagitated response to attacks on him and his theology just beginning to be made by incoming missionaries. They are "peddlars of God's word" (2:17), men who make money by selling their preaching.

3:1-6 begins Paul's defense. Paul's opponents must have paraded their own "*letters of recommendation*" and *respect for Moses* (tables of stone) as a validating contrast to Paul. Paul's answer is that the Christian community of Corinth is all the validation he needs and that Christian instruction has been written on their hearts by the Spirit. It is the new covenant (v. 6) of Jeremiah 31:31 that Paul heralds, a covenant energized by the life-giving Spirit rather than by the death-dealing written code.

3:7-18. This new covenant surpasses even the splendor of the old. Moses had to veil his face to shield his followers from the divine splendor. He and his writings still remain veiled except through Christ in whom we can now behold the divine glory and be changed gradually into his likeness (eikona, v. 18) from one degree to another. Christian salvation, says Paul, consists in our being changed ever more into Christ's living icons (v. 18). As Jesus is the icon of the Father, we are enabled in the Spirit to be icons of Jesus.

4:1-6. Paul's opening verses must be in answer to accusations against him. He is not underhanded, cunning, one who tampers with God's word, nor is his good news veiled/mystifying except for those blinded from seeing that Jesus is the icon of God (v. 4). Paul's creed is simple: Jesus Christ is Lord (v. 5 and cf. Phil 2:11; Rom 10:9); Paul is his servant. V. 6 may refer to Paul's conversion and to the foundation of his Christ-centered theology; Paul has seen "the glory of God in the face of Christ" (v. 6).

4:7-15. Paul contrasts his own weakness to his opponents' show of strength. As an earthen vessel (v. 7), he, like Jesus before him, demonstrates God's exclusive power. Jesus' human weakness led to death and resurrection, and so will that of Paul and all Christians (v. 14). Human weakness coupled to divine strength is the force behind true missionary work.

4:16-5:10. Paul presents to us an inspiring goal. He asks us to compare the inferior present to the inspiring future, setting as opposites:

> earthly tent----------------eternal building in the heavens
> clothed ---------------------further clothed
> mortal ----------------------life
> home in body--------------in Lord
> faith-------------------------sight
> in the body-----------------home with the Lord.

Of this inspiring future, the present gift of the Spirit is the *arrabōn* (5:5), the initial payment which guarantees the whole. That is, if we live and act as Christians, for we shall be judged by our works (5:10).

5:11-21 is a powerful piece of Pauline theology. The love of Christ (v. 14) his for us, ours for him, is the controlling factor. Jesus' love was manifest especially in his death, *a death for others*. So, too, as the heart of Paul's ideal for humanity, we are called to live, no longer for ourselves, but for another, for Christ (v. 15). Christian maturity is to surpass self-centered love to be able to live and die for others.

This new vision/possibility for humanity is a thumbnail sketch of the newness of life, the new creation, which reconciliation has produced. Of this, God is the cause, God reconciles us (v. 18). The description is not that of humanity reconciling an angry God, but of a loving God drawing errant humanity back through love in Christ. God, in Christ, shows us what it means to say that humanity is God's image, by describing true life as that which is lived not for ourselves. Not only does Jesus' life and death give us the picture of what real humanity should be, it also gives us the power to match up to the pattern. We do have the Spirit, the *arrabōn* (v. 5); we are a "new creation" (v. 17). Gifts confer responsibility, and so, we, too, are called to be ministers of reconciliation. Can we, through our lives and deaths, be God's appeal in Christ so that others "might live no longer for themselves" (5:15)?

6:1-10 is a paragraph devoted to a defense of Paul's ministry. He not only preaches Christ crucified (1:22), he also imitates him (vv. 3-5). Paul's life of suffering stems from his dedication (vv. 6-8). Christ's life led to his passion; so does Paul's.

6:11-13; 7:2-4 conclude this letter of defense (B). Paul states his openness to the Corinthians and his love for them. He begs, in return, that they open wide their hearts to him.

(C) 6:14-7:1. This short section breaks the continuity between what precedes and what follows (cf. 6:11-13 and 7:2-4). A number of scholars believe that the editor of 2 Cor inserted this section, not Pauline, into the composition. Its language of polarities resembles a similar strain in the writings of the Dead Sea community. Other scholars believe that the editor adjoined here a genuine scrap from Paul's lost letter referred to in 1 Cor 5:9-13 where Paul says, "I wrote to you in my letter not to associate with immoral men, etc." This teaching is certainly similar to what is found here in 2 Cor 6:14-7:1.

(7:5-16 treated above after 2:13.)

(D) 8:1-24 deals exclusively with the collection for Jerusalem which became such an important project for Paul. By it he hoped to convince the Jewish Christians of Jerusalem of the loyalty and love which the Pauline Churches had in their regard. He may also have seen his projected procession of Gentile Christians (cf. Acts 20:4) bearing gifts to Jerusalem as the eschatological fulfillment of Is 2:2-3; Micah 4:1-2. Titus (v. 6) will be Paul's responsible "partner and fellow worker" (v. 23). He will be assisted by two unnamed assistants, "the brother who is famous among all the churches for his preaching of the gospel" (v. 18) and "our brother whom we have often tested and found earnest in many matters (v. 22). Who these two helpers are is impossible to determine. Guesses always seem to involve Luke in some fashion.

There are two powerful statements in this section. One concerns Paul's concept of Christian sharing (vv. 13-14). By fostering this collection, Paul does not intend to burden the Corinthians. Rather, he hopes simply that what they have extra can satisfy Jerusalem's wants now. Perhaps the positions will be reversed in the future. A basic equality is a goal to strive for. A second statement concerns Jesus who "though he was rich, yet for your sake he became poor, so that by his poverty you might become rich" (v. 9). Christ's movement from richness to poverty parallels that of Phil 2:6-8 where Jesus empties himself and proceeds to crucifixion. Paul's statement here in 2 Cor 8:9 certainly seems to presume Jesus' preexistence and heavenly riches.

(E) 9:1-15. Some commentators believe that c. 9 is simply a continuation of the note on the collection contained in c. 8, and that "the brethren" of 9:5 are those assistants already referred to in 8:18, 22. But even these authors admit the jarring connection between the two. More probably, c. 9 is a different letter of commendation for others of Paul's assistants (vv. 3, 5) as they organize the collection, not exclusively in Corinth (c. 8) but in the other Christian churches of Achaia (9:2).

(F) 10:1-13:14 is Paul's anguished defense of his own ministry. It is most often identified as the *letter of tears* mentioned in 2 Cor 2:3-4; 7:8. Chronologically speaking, it appears to follow after Paul's second—and painful—visit, which came after the calm defense of 2 Cor 2:14-7:4 (B), which, itself, followed 1 Cor. Its tone is quite different from anything else in this letter. Paul's relationship with the church at Corinth is at issue. "Super-apostles" (11:5; 12:11) have entered the community with conceited claims for themselves, i.e. that they are truly Jewish, powerful in deeds, ecstatic—and with sharp criticism of Paul. He had carried no letters of recommendation from the Jerusalem authorities; he had not merited financial support from the Corinthians; though a decisive letter writer, he was a weak speaker. It is this sharp criticism that provokes Paul's extremely personal defense. Presumably Titus is carrying this letter which will prove so effective that he, Titus, can later report to Paul that peace had settled both on the Corinthian Christians and on their relationship to their founding apostle. The original introduction to this letter has not been utilized because the letter itself—or a good piece of it—has been incorporated into this larger synthetic 2 Corinthians.

10:1-18. Paul's approach in this chapter is tentative. He has been criticized for being a powerful letter writer but considerably weaker when physically present (vv. 1, 10). How can one respond to such criticism? For the moment Paul must be content to say that he will, if necessary, exercise his authority "for building you up and not for destroying you" (v. 8) when he returns to Corinth. But he hopes that this will not be necessary. There is a slight indication of who the adversaries are in v. 7's "If anyone is confident that he is Christ's..." This is reminiscent of the fourth faction of 1 Cor 1:12, "I belong to Christ," and seems to refer to a particularly ecstatic/enthusiastic group which affirms direct, charismatic, elitist union with the Lord. This insistence may account for Paul's extraordinary description of his own special ecstatic revelation in 12:1-11. Throughout this section Paul is being led into discussions and affirmations that he really would prefer to avoid. He writes with a sort of half-willing reluctance (12:11), being forced to toot his own horn while realizing that such a melody is always off key.

11:1-12:13. This section is a mixture of slight attack and strong defense. Paul confronts his opponents (11:1-6, 12-21a) without giving many specifics, except that he sees them as taking advantage of the Corinthian Christians who are said to cower before them (11:19-20). His main attitude, however, is one of defense. He defends his refusal to accept money from his converts (11:7-11), while noting that, in this regard, the Macedonians (cf. also Phil 4:14-18) have been an exception (v. 9). He describes his missionary sufferings at length (11:21b-33), giving details unknown to us from Luke's account in Acts. He even describes an ecstatic experience (12:1-6). Fittingly, he concludes with an insistence on his own weakness (12:7-10) and with an apology (12:11-13) for whatever boasting he has felt constrained to do.

12:14-13:10. Paul is about ready to visit the Corinthians for the third time (12:14; 13:1). He makes avowal of his love with, perhaps, a denial that he has been crafty in the use of money. (Has he been accused by some of skimming off some of the collection?) Titus, too, has been scrupulously honest (12:14-18).

Paul hopes so much that his coming visit will be effected in peace, without disappointment on either side (12:19-21). This third visit will be like the two-three witnesses (13:1) required by Jewish law. He hopes that he will be spared the necessity of having the divine disciplinary power work through his confessed weakness (13:1-4). May the Corinthians act as true Christians in whom Jesus Christ dwells. Paul insists that he does have divine authority, but that it is (as in 10:8) "for building up and not for tearing down" (13:5-10).

13:11-14. Paul's conclusion is a deeply felt appeal for peace: "live in peace and the God of . . . peace will be with you" (v. 11). It is as though the difficulty with factions in Corinth with which Paul began I Cor has resurfaced to overshadow 2 Cor as well. "Factionalism" is the literary inclusion of 1-2 Corinthians. Paul's final words in v. 14 are strikingly Trinitarian. He calls down the blessing of the Lord Jesus, God, and the Holy Spirit.

## 3. SOME OF THIS LETTER'S HIGH POINTS

Though it is somewhat distracting for today's reader to analyze a letter originating from different moments in Paul's sometimes stormy relationship with the Corinthians, we must be grateful to the editor—presumed—who saved these various passages for us. They have enabled us to acquire new and valuable insights into friend Paul.

a) The letter of comfort (A = 1:1-2:13, plus 7:5-16) bares Paul's humanity. He is delighted at the successful conclusion of this personal conflict. The battle is o'er, peace is won. Paul who departed from Ephesus with a heavy heart, and who was deeply disturbed not to find Titus at Troas, is now rejoicing to have found him in Macedonia as bearer of good news (2:12-13; 7:5-7).

b) Paul has developed in his mild defense (2:14-7:4) a truly magnificent theology of reconciliation. It speaks of God's love to be accepted, not of God's wrath to be feared. This reconciling love is offered in and through Christ who is God's icon, expressing in his life and death what it means to be God and what it means to be truly human. We are called to live, not for ourselves but for Christ and for each other. The Spirit makes this possible. Reconciliation encompasses God's love, expressed in Jesus, who shows us how to live and gives us the Spirit-strength to accomplish this. In Jesus, the divine icon, we become God's icons, too, spreading the work of reconciliation in the world.

c) Part of Paul's icon life is spelled out for us in the explicit biographical details of 11:22-33. There is no limit to Paul's endeavors, no suffering too great as he lives and dies for others. This is an insight into Paul who reveals Christ who reveals God.

d) But Christian life is not all agony by any means. The following chapter 12 gives us a view into the ecstasy as well, Paul caught up into Paradise, hearing words "that cannot be told, which man may not utter" (12:4). Paul's life, like that of the Jesus he follows, is an epitome of Christian living.

## Recommended Readings

C.K. Barrett, *The Second Epistle to the Corinthians* (Harper & Row, 1973). This is another of Barrett's excellent contributions to biblical study. It contains a first-rate commentary and a more than adequate introduction. Barrett postulates a union of only two Pauline letters found in the material now contained in cc. 1-9 and 10-13.

P. Ellis, *Seven Pauline Letters,* 139-172, is rather unique in viewing 2 Cor as a unity which follows, again, Paul's A-B-A format.

M.A. Getty has been referred to when speaking of her offering in the CBC series, #8. She hesitates to determine how many of Paul's writings have been united to form this one letter, but accepts some kind of editorial unification. Her introduction, exegesis and format are appealing.

# 6

# Paul's Letter to the Philippians

## 1. HISTORICAL BACKGROUND

Acts 16 provides a lively description of the founding of the Philippian church. It is Paul's second journey; he is accompanied by at least Silas (Acts 15:40) and Timothy (Acts 16:1-4). Luke also may be present, since it is precisely at this point (Acts 16:10) that the text, abruptly and unexpectedly, begins to employ the first person plural "we". This is the first of the so-called "we sections". The church in Philippi, Paul's first founding in Europe, was initially centered around Lydia and her home which, undoubtedly, became Paul's house-church (Acts 16:15). Lydia was both a businesswoman and a Gentile "god-fearer" (Acts 16:14). So loving was her relationship with Paul that, as the apostle leaves the city in haste after a brief imprisonment, he still takes time to visit her for a fond farewell (Acts 16:40). Paul's relationship to this whole church was warm and personal. It is the only church from which Paul accepted charity (Phil 1:5; 4:10-18; 2 Cor 11:9), thus breaking away from his usual insistence on self-support (1 Thess 2:5-9; 2 Thess 3:7-9; 1 Cor 9:4-18; 2 Cor 11:7-10).

## 2. LITERARY BACKGROUND

There are two difficult questions regarding the origin of this letter, one concerning its unity, the other its place of composition.

a) Unity. There is lively discussion regarding the unity of Philippians. A number of scholars believe that Phil, like 2 Cor, has been fashioned together from what were originally independent writings. They point to the sharp break at 3:2 as proof-positive of a section that is only artificially connected with what has preceded. There is further suggestion that 4:10ff was originally an independent letter of thanksgiving for the gift sent to Paul via Epaphroditus. This would add up to three separate writings placed into unity by an editor:

> 1:1-3:1;
> 3:2-4:9;
> 4:10-23.

Although this opinion has strong arguments in its favor, I believe that Philippians is, and has always been, a single letter. 1:5 is the thanksgiving's early reference both to the gift brought by Epaphroditus in 4:18 and to the Philippian partnership with Paul of 4:15-16. As we have already experienced, Paul's thanksgivings give a brief preview of what is to come. In this case c. 1 is already looking forward to the material of c. 4. And 3:20-21 is intimately connected to 2:5-11. What happens to the exalted Christ in 2:9-11 will be the lot of all Christians in 3:20-21. This latter passage is connected to the former in both terminology and theological concept.

b) Place of origin is a second major introductory problem with Philippians. The text itself speaks of imprisonment (1:7, 13-14, 17), and the general view over the centuries has been that Phil was composed during Paul's Roman imprisonment in the early 60's. But a fair amount of evidence points in a different direction.

i—The letter supposes frequent communication between Philippi and Paul, and this favors (but doesn't necessarily prove) a site of imprisonment closer to Philippi than Rome. Thus

-news of Paul's imprisonment is carried to Philippi;
-Epaphroditus goes from Philippi to Paul (4:18);
-news of Epaphroditus' illness moves back to Philippi (2:26);
-news of Philippians' distress is communicated to Paul (2:28).

This multiple intercommunication argues more toward an undocumented Asian-Ephesian imprisonment (cf. 1 Cor 15:30-32; 2 Cor 1:8-10; Acts 19:23-41) than a Roman locale. The trip from Philippi to Rome was approximately five times as long as that from Philippi to Ephesus, c. five weeks of travel as opposed to one.

ii—Paul speaks in Phil 2:24 of his hope to visit Philippi shortly. But if he were writing from Rome, would he not be thinking of going west, not east, after his release, as indicated in his stated plan to move on from Rome to Spain (Rom 15:28)? This argument, however, is weak since it presumes that Paul's determination c. 58 AD to go westward to Spain remained constant during his subsequent *4 years* of imprisonment in Caesarea and Rome. How many things could have occurred in the meanwhile to have changed his plans!

iii—The content of Phil agrees more with that of Paul's great letters (1-2 Cor, Gal, Rom) than it does with Colossians, which I consider of Roman origin. Phil 3:9, in particular, is a one-verse miniature of both Galatians and Romans.

iv—Note how 2 Cor 11:9's "my needs were supplied by the brethren who came from Macedonia" may well refer to the same circumstances as those of Phil 4:10-18. If so, this would place the composition of Phil 4 close to the time of 2 Cor 11, and would argue in favor of an Asian-Ephesian rather than Roman composition of Philippians.

For these reasons I favor an Ephesian composition written during an imprisonment of which Luke makes no mention in Acts. The letter, then, would have been written during Paul's third journey about the same time as I Cor and before the final pieces of II Cor written after Paul had left Ephesus for Troas and Macedonia.

## 3. IMMEDIATE PREPARATION

Read Acts 16 for Luke's description of Paul's founding visit to Philippi. Note how this fits into the overall itinerary of the second journey. Read and reread, in a small group when possible, Philippians itself. Do you note any intolerable breaks in continuity?

## 4. PHILIPPIANS ACCORDING TO PAUL'S CUSTOMARY LITERARY FORMAT

*a) Introduction (1:1-2).*

Senders = Paul and Timothy. There is no note of authority here. Paul and Timothy are simply "servants of Christ Jesus."

Addressees = the saints, the chosen ones, at Philippi, together with the bishops (episkopois) and deacons (diakonois). Whereas there was little or no reference in the Corinthian correspondence to church hierarchical structure (cf. however 1 Cor 12:28), here in Phil we have immediate reference to both bishops (the original Greek means simply supervisors or superintendents) and deacons. Some commentators believe this is non-Pauline and speak of a later interpolation into the text. Better to accept the text as it is and recognize that the Pauline churches, too, demanded at least a minimum structure to hold them together as sociological units. The letter of recommendation for Phoebe, the deaconess, in Romans 16 is further proof of offices within the Pauline churches.

Greeting: again, "grace...and peace".

*b) Thanksgiving (1:3-11)*

Paul's love for the Philippians strains his vocabulary. In his *every* prayer, for *all* of them Paul holds them in his heart (v. 7), yearning for them all "with the affection of Christ

Jesus" (v. 8). Already in the thanksgiving we note the appearance of two concepts which will be important for the rest of the letter, Paul's overwhelming joy (v. 4) and the Philippians' partnership with him in the spreading of the good news.

### c) Body (1:12-3:21)

1:12-26 spells out Paul's situation. He doesn't tell us where he is—the Philippians already know that—but he speaks repeatedly of his imprisonment (vv. 13, 14, 17). This imprisonment has turned into a source of joy because other Christians have been influenced by it to preach Christ more vigorously (vv. 14-18). Paul's captivity has given him time and reason to think about possible death. He's ready to die, his bags are packed: "My desire is to depart and be with Christ, for that is far better" (v. 23). Yet he is convinced that his life will be spared for others' progress and joy in the faith. He expects to see the Philippians again (vv. 25-26).

1:27-2:18. In the meantime Paul has some advice for these loved Christians. He wants them to be united, to "stand firm in one spirit, with one mind striving side by side for the faith of the Gospel" (1:27). He wants them to be "of the same mind, having the same love, being in full accord and of one mind" (2:2). Such unity demands mutual humility, and here Paul has a model to offer (vv. 5-11), Christ who emptied himself, becoming a servant, a human being, obedient to death even to crucifixion. In response, God has exalted him and given him a name that merits divine worship, for Jesus Christ is LORD. This primitive hymn—probably anterior to its Pauline usage at this point—is a powerful expression of faith in the preexistence, human existence and glorified postexistence of Jesus Christ. It has been a source of Christian faith, challenge and dogma over the centuries.

It is the example of Christ that the Philippians are called to follow. If they do, they will be light to a darkened world (v. 15, and cf. Mt. 5:14-16; Jn 9:5), a proof that Paul has not labored in vain.

2:19-30 give travel news. Paul expects to send Timothy to

Philippi as soon as his own fate is more determined. Timothy will then be able to pass along the latest news concerning this prisoner for Christ. Paul hopes that even he, too, will soon be able to visit this loved Church (v. 24).

Epaphroditus will definitely be heading off. Recovered now from a near fatal sickness, his return will bring joy to his worried friends in Philippi. Presumably he will be carrying this letter with him.

3:1-11 constitute a definite problem. Paul's use of "Finally" (3:1) usually introduces a conclusion, a winding-down of the letter. But, instead, Paul takes off in v. 2 with a strong attack on "those who mutilate the flesh," on those, surely, who advocate a Christian Judaism with insistence on circumcision and the Law. Seemingly, these Mosaic elements are being proposed as essential, and Paul cannot abide this betrayal of the good news. As a Benjaminite, a Hebrew, a Pharisee, a past persecutor, a blameless observer of the Law, he knows and has lived these Jewish elements, but they are no longer of salvific value for a follower of Christ. Paul seeks not "a righteousness of (his) own, based on law, but that which is through faith in Christ, the righteousness from God that depends on faith" (v. 9). This expresses the main theme of Galatians and Romans, a defense of Gentile Christianity independent from the legal observances of the Judaism from which Paul took origin. Paul's doctrine builds on a faith acceptance of Christ, of Christ who passed from suffering to resurrection. This passage from death to life is, for us Christians, a present and future possiblility.

3:12-21. Not that Paul has already made perfect passage. He, too, is in process; God has not finished with him yet. "I press on toward the goal for the prize of the upward call of God in Christ Jesus (v. 14). There are others—perhaps Christians themselves—who have taken a detour. "Their end is destruction, their God is the belly, and they glory in their shame, with minds set on earthly things" (v. 19). This appears to be a group other than the sympathizers with Judaism, a group for whom sexual conduct is of small consequence. Paul's thoughts and hopes frame a different ideal. As Jesus was exalted, glorified and transformed in 2:9-11, so shall we, by his power and through this same Lord Jesus, be changed into the glory that is his (vv. 20-21). The divine has become human to make the human divine.

## d) Exhortation (4:1-20)

4:1-3. Euodia and Syntyche are asked to settle their grievance. A "true yokefellow" (v. 3) is asked to help as peacemaker. These women have been Paul's co-workers, part of an extensive legion of important Christian women including Priscilla, Phoebe the deaconess and, with her, the long list of women whom Paul eulogizes in Romans 16.

4:4-7. Rejoice, rejoice. Pray, be thankful, be at peace— the Lord is at hand.

4:8-9. This is a rare view of Paul the humanist. Concentrate on whatever is true, honorable, just, pure, lovely, gracious, excellent, whatever is worthy of praise.

4:10-20 is a final reference to the Philippians' past and present support of Paul and his work. No sooner had he left Philippi for Thessalonica (Acts 17:1), than they had sent help "once and again" (4:16). And now they have sent more help by way of Epaphroditus, "a fragrant offering, a sacrifice acceptable and pleasing to God" (v. 18). Paul has learned by experience not to complain, to endure both hunger and want (vv. 11-12). How nice to see the other side of the coin on occasion!

## e) Conclusion (4:21-23)

Paul sends greetings from all Christians who are with him, "especially those of Caesar's household." This might refer to *Roman* Christians, but need not. Members of Caesar's household would be found in every Roman enclave as residents and workers in the local Roman administrative center. Philippi itself had become a Roman colony after Anthony and Octavian had defeated Brutus and Cassius in the battle of Philippi (42 B.C.).

Paul's final wish for the Philippians is "Grace." May they be filled with every good gift of God.

## 5. PARTICULAR OBSERVATIONS

a) The "bishops and deacons" of 1:1. There is no manuscript evidence that points to this phrase as being a later interpolation. It is better to accept the phrase as it stands, a clear indication of an incipient hierarchy in this Pauline church. This should make us hesitant to judge that any Pauline community, even that of Corinth, depended solely on occasional charismatic leadership. (Cf. also 1 Thess 5:12-13; Rom 12:8; 1 Cor 12:28.) At the same time, it is anachronous to translate *episkopois* as "bishops," if this latter term evokes the full panoply of later episcopacy. It is evident from other N.T. texts that episkopoi (supervisors) and presbuteroi (elders) were used synonymously at this period. In Acts 20:17, for example, Paul summons the "presbuteroi". In Acts 20:28 he calls these same people "episkopoi". 1 Peter 5:1-2, appealing to "presbuteroi," tells them to fulfill the office of episkopoi." Titus 1:5-7 uses "presbuteros" and "episkopos" as synonyms. The traditional tri-level hierarchy of bishop-priest (presbuteros)-deacon, however, is clearly attested at the beginning of the second century in the writings of Ignatius of Antioch (c. 110 A.D.). (Cf. Magnesians 2 and 6; Trallians 3 and 7; Philadelphians 4; Smyrnaeans 8; Polycarp 6.)

b) Joy. It is part of a Christian paradox that this letter, which clearly alludes to Paul's imprisonment (1:7, 13, 14, 17), is precisely the letter in which Paul insists so repeatedly on Christian joy. No less than sixteen times (1:4, 18$^2$, 25; 2:2, 17$^2$, 18$^2$, 19, 28, 29; 3:1; 4:4$^2$, 10) does Paul encourage his readers to make joy a central emotion in their lives. They were to be alleluia people. Even if we were to dissect this letter into various parts, as suggested by many scholars, we would still have 1:1-3:1 as a unit, with 13 instances of Paul's call for joy in the Lord.

c) Christological hymn of 2:5-11. This text, without doubt, has been one of the most important christological passages in the history of Christendom. It probably existed even anterior to its use here by Paul since v. 9 omits any mention of Jesus' resurrection—and it's hard to imagine

Paul doing that—to pass directly from death to exaltation. This would mean that the hymn may have been composed as early as the 40's.

There is abundant discussion today as to the type of christology the hymn is proposing. Two explanations are most prominent.

i—The hymn does not speak of a divine preexistence on the part of Christ. It says, rather, that the human Jesus, made in the image of God, (like all descendants of Adam), did not commit the Adamic sin of blasphemous claim to divine equality but, rather, accepted the role of a human servant who, in obedience, humbled himself to death, even death on a cross. In this explanation there is no divine preexistence, and the theological point is a comparison between Adam's blasphemous pretensions and Jesus' obedient humility. Jesus' earthly existence was capped by supreme humiliation and followed by a glorification in which Jesus is declared Lord to whom is given the use of God's name as an instrument of power. Divine preexistence is neither claimed nor implied.

ii—The traditional explanation of this section sees a much higher christology involved. It believes that the hymn, and Paul who adopts it, speaks of a heavenly preexistence followed by an earthly existence of obedient humility, followed by a heavenly exaltation. Jesus, who in preexistent form was equal with God, emptied himself of all divine appearance—transfiguration in reverse, as it is often said— to live as a human being, perfect in humble obedience (as Adam was not). As a consequence, he becomes, even in exalted *humanity*, supreme Lord to whom every knee should bend and every tongue proclaim. I believe that this is the high christology which both the hymn and Paul present. Note how the content of this passage is paralleled by Paul in 2 Cor 8:9's, "For you know the grace of our *Lord Jesus* Christ, that though he was rich, yet for your sake he became poor, so that by his poverty you might become rich." In content, this Pauline creation is a combination of the ideas of Phil 2:6-11 and 3:20-21, i.e., it expresses both the abasement of Christ and the glorification of Christians. More to the point, its statement that Jesus, *who was rich*, became poor for our sake seems to demand a preexistence of richness. Moreover, Jesus' postexistence in Phil 2:9-11 is on such a divine level that it is more logically explained if it follows upon a divine preexistence. Phil 2:10 attributes to the postexistent Jesus the phraseology used of God/Yahweh in Isaiah 45:23 and, by Paul himself, in Rom 14:11. And the name-theology of Phil 2:9-10 refers to Jesus the powerful God-statement of Isaiah 42:8; "I am the Lord, that is my name; my glory I give to no other." Philippian's strong God-references to Jesus in 2:9-11 make it more probable that vv. 6-7 refer, also, to a divine existence on the part of Jesus. Schematically, therefore, Phil and Paul see Jesus as model in these stages:

heavenly preexistence                    heavenly exaltation
                    ↘ earthly humiliation ↗

This explanation, however, does agree with the other in acknowledging an Adamic overtone. Jesus is contrasted to Adam who, unlike Jesus, made false claim to divinity. Jesus not only made no such *false* claim, he even gave up every form of divine appearance.

One final note: behind Phil 2:5-11 lie both the theology and vocabulary of the suffering servant of Is 52:13-53:12 who, though a man of sorrows and grief, poured out his soul to death and was, consequently, exalted and given a portion with the mighty.

d) The break at 3:1-2. It is certainly true that 3:2 comes so abruptly and unexpectedly that its shift in subject constitutes a solid argument for proposing here an unsuccessful knitting of two different documents. I have already argued in the opposite direction, that is, that Philippians is, and has always been, one unified letter. This leaves me with the difficulty of explaining why it is that 3:2 is so awkwardly situated. There is no evident response. My own suggestion is that Paul, at this point, did intend to conclude his letter— and thus the "finally" of 3:1 which may have intended originally to pass on to the material of 4:8ff, or 4:10ff. But the letter was interrupted for a period of time, not necessarily long, during which Paul received news of the Christian Jewish movement which so disturbed him in 3:2. Such an interruption may seem like a *Deus ex machina*, but interruptions were inevitable in Paul's era when writing was so physically arduous and prolonged.

e) Biographical details of Phil 3:5-6. Though this whole chapter is an unexpected element in Paul's letter, it offers valuable material for filling out our picture of the historical Paul. " . . . circumcised on the eighth day, of the people of Israel, of the tribe of Benjamin, a Hebrew born of Hebrews; as to the law a Pharisee, as to zeal a persecutor of the church, as to righteousness under the law blameless." This is the pre-Christian, Benjaminite Saul, rooted in every sense in his Jewish origins, blameless in his obedience to the law, zealous persecutor of the church.

f) True yokefellow of 4:3. It is impossible to determine who this person is. That impossibility, however, has not kept scholars from guessing. The reference, e.g. could be to Luke if, as one could argue from the temporary cessation of the "we-section" after Acts 16, he had been left behind in Philippi till picked up again by Paul some years later on Paul's collection trip to Jerusalem (Acts 20:6). Although the phrase is in the masculine, this has not prevented some ancient commentators such as Origen and Clement of Alexandria from suggesting that Paul is referring at this point to his wife. The French author, Renan, identified her as Lydia. But such exciting possibilities seem nullified by Paul's own statement in 1 Cor 7:8 that he is celibate and quite determined to remain so.

## Recommended Readings

Four practical commentaries on this letter can be found in:
P. Ellis, *Seven Pauline Letters* (1982), 115-138 which also offers an excellent excursus on the christological hymn of 2:6-11;

M.A. Getty, *Philippians and Philemon* (Glazier, NT message #14, 1980) suggests Ephesus as Philippians' place of origin, while giving a good popular exposition of the letter;

J. Houlden, *Paul's Letters from Prison* (Westminster, 1970), 31-116, the work of an expert who knows how to combine brevity with scholarship;

R. Martin, *Philippians* (Eerdmans, 1980)

Further discussion on the christological content of Phil 2:6-11 is offered by:

G. Howard, "Phil 2:6-11 and the Human Christ," *CBQ* 40 (July 1978), 368-387;

J. Murphy-O'Connor, "Christological Anthropology in Phil., II, 6-11," *Revue Biblique* 83 (1976), 25-50;

C.H. Talbert, "The Problem of Pre-Existence in Phil 2:6-11," *JBL* 86 (1967), 141-153.

All three of these authors agree in denying any affirmation of Christ's divine preexistence in this hymn. Contrary opinions can be found in most other commentaries on this passage.

# 7

# Paul's Letter to the Galatians

## 1. HISTORICAL BACKGROUND

It is strange that this letter, so definitely Paul's and so completely filled with his theology, cannot be clearly located. We are not sure where Paul wrote it, nor where the churches were to which Paul sent it. The address (1:2) is brief, cool and ambiguous: "To the churches of Galatia." No other help is available in the letter. But addressing the churches of Galatia at that time was like addressing the churches of New York today. Which New York—the city or the state? Which Galatia—the ancient kingdom of the Galli (Gauls) in northern Asia Minor, or the much extended Roman province which included, in the south, the cities which Paul and Barnabas had visited (e.g. Pisidian Antioch, Iconium, Lystra, Derbe) on their first journey? The fact that Paul calls his addressees "Galatai-Galatians" in 3:1 leads me to believe that he writes to the true Galatai of the north, in which case he would have visited them, not on the first voyage, but on both the second (Acts 16:6) and third (Acts 18:23). The content and style of Galatians corresponds much more with those of 1-2 Cor and Rom than with the earlier 1-2 Thess or later Col/Eph, so I would date it c. 56-57, a bit ahead of Romans. It may have been written from Ephesus or Macedonia before Paul's third trip to Corinth (Acts 20:1-3) from which he wrote Romans.

## 2. IMMEDIATE PREPARATION

Read and reread Galatians aloud. What is its emotional tone? Are there any passages of tenderness? How does Paul feel at the beginning, during, and at the end of the letter?

## 3. GALATIANS ACCORDING TO PAUL'S CUSTOMARY LITERARY FORMAT

Paul's emotional level is so high throughout the letter that the formalized literary divisions are somewhat obliterated. It is especially difficult to determine exactly where the body ends and the exhortation begins. Yet the literary pattern does exist.

### a) *Introduction (1:1-5)*

Sender—only Paul is mentioned by name. He introduces himself with all the authority at his command. No longer the simple servant of Christ Jesus (as in Phil 1:1), Paul is apostle, not by some human choice but by the design of Jesus and of God the Father who raised him from the dead. Paul appears in full uniform, with all his medals attached.

Addressees = "the churches of Galatia." No flourish is added, the address is brief and dry.

Greetings = "grace and peace" as usual, but with an introduction already of Paul's mighty theme, that we are delivered by Jesus (and only by Jesus) "who gave himself for our sins." What law was and is unable to do, Jesus did and does.

### b) *Thanksgiving.*

*There is none!* Paul is so disturbed, agitated, and angry that he is unable to feign a literary pretext. He is *not* thankful for what is happening in the Galatian churches, and refuses to pretend that he is. In no other Pauline letter is the thanksgiving missing except, seemingly, in Ephesians where, however, the long blessing of 1:3-14 constitutes a splendid and fitting substitute.

*c) Body (1:6-4:31)*

1:6-2:10 is Paul's defense of his gospel, his apostleship and his mission. Clearly, all of these elements have been attacked in Galatia by Christians who believe that Paul has deformed the gospel message, is simply a second-rate preacher dependent on the major apostles, and with no legitimate mission to the Gentiles. Paul's entire work among the Galatian churches is being vilified. He reacts with vigor.

i — 1:6-10. The good news, the *only* good news is that which Paul has preached to them. There is no other, and any one who would preach differently should be set aside, anathematized.

ii — 1:11-24. Paul's apostleship is not second-class, completely dependent on conferral and validation by the major apostles. Paul's calling — like that of the other apostles —has come from Jesus (v. 12) who summoned Paul from his Judaic past to preach among the Gentiles. His conversion to Christ was so completely Jesus-controlled that it led to no immediate contact at all with the apostles. Rather, like the God-summoned prophets of the past (note how v. 15 echoes Is 49:1 and Jer 1:5), Paul moved out into the wilderness of Arabia, and then on to Damascus (v. 17).

Only three years later did Paul have any initial contact with the apostles. He visited Cephas in Jerusalem for two weeks (v. 18). What one would give for a tape recording of their conversations! But even there his contact with the apostles was limited, for he met no other apostles, though he did see James, the Lord's brother. (The Greek does not permit us to judge whether Paul considered James an apostle or not.) Then off he went to Syria (Antioch) and Cilicia (Tarsus) leaving the Judean churches in amazement at his change from persecutor to propagator.

iii — With regard to Paul's mission to the Gentiles (2:1-

10), that was solemnly confirmed fourteen years later in open meeting with those who were considered the very pillars of the church — James, Cephas and John. The occasion was a trip to Jerusalem by Paul, Barnabas and Titus to discuss freedom and bondage within the church (v. 4). Freedom won out. Titus, a Greek, was not bound to circumcision but declared free from it, and Paul was recognized as "entrusted with the gospel to the uncircumcised, just as Peter had been entrusted with the gospel to the circumcised" (v. 7). The only request made of Paul was that he and his churches remember the poor, a request to which Paul acceded eagerly. Much of his time, energy and letters would be devoted to this very activity (1 Cor 16:1-4; 2 Cor 8-9; Rom 15:25-28).

2:11-3:29 circles and recircles around *the good news, the gospel*, to which Paul referred so often in 1:6-11.

— i — 2:11-21, confrontation with Cephas in Antioch. Paul presents the good news within an historical setting, his vivid disappointment with the conduct of Peter, other Jewish Christians and even Barnabas. Previously willing to break bread with the Gentiles, they had separated from them at the insistence of the "circumcision party" (v. 12) as though the kosher prescriptions of the law were more essential than Christian unity and equality. This, for Paul, was not the good news "that a man is not justified by works of the law but through faith in Jesus Christ; even we have believed in Christ Jesus, in order to be justified by faith in Christ, and not by works of the law, because by works of the law shall no one be justified" (v. 16). Paul's gospel to the Gentiles is that they were on equal footing with their Jewish Christian brothers and sisters — eating together signifies that, eating apart denies it. This is the good news, the only good news, and Paul will stand up to anyone who perverts it. Law is not essential, only Christ is, and Christ is available equally to Jew and Gentile. That is the Christian gospel and it means, for Paul personally, that "it is no longer I who live, but Christ who lives in me; and the life I now live in the flesh I live by faith in the Son of God, who loved me and gave himself for me" (v. 20).

— ii — 3:1-5. Paul argues for the good news of equal justification by faith, free from law, by appealing to the Galatians' personal experience. The Spirit had been a felt reality in their lives, as had miracles. And this before this recent emergence of the doctrine of law as essential. But if both Spirit and mighty works had been evident apart from the law, how could law itself be essential?

— iii — 3:6-9. And what about Abraham who was justified because he believed, and in whom, and through whose example, all would be blessed? His had been a faith justification. Thus it is the faith-Christians, not the law-Christians, who would be blessed with Abraham. Paul, apostle to the uncircumcised (2:9), wages battle for the Christian equality of all Gentile converts.

— iv — 3:10-29. But if all this is true, "Why then the law?" (v. 19). Paul embarks upon an argument to which he will later return in Romans 7. The law had come from God —Paul is not even tempted to deny that — but why? What purpose did it serve?

At this point, Paul's presentation becomes difficult, tortuous, as though — and it's probably true — he was working with a problem to which he did not see a totally satisfying solution. He begins (vv. 10-14) by noting that the law could be considered a negative factor, a curse, because it set up demands which people were unable to fulfill, with punishment for non-fulfillment. But Christ, figuratively speaking, nailed this curse to the cross with his own death, a death which, according to Dt 21:22-23, was a veritable curse. He adds (vv. 15-18) the point that the law did not remove or annul the promise made to Abraham 430 years earlier, the promise that uncircumcised Gentiles would inherit a blessing in his name. This they did in Christ, Abraham's unique offspring. Only at this juncture (vv. 19-25) does Paul cautiously attempt to position the law. Why the law? "It was added because of transgressions" is Paul's ambiguous answer (v. 19). Paul's meaning will become clearer in Romans, but it is surely vague at this point. The commands of law set up the conditions for transgressions, and people were too weak to obey. Law led, therefore, to transgressions from which Jesus saves those who believe in faith (v. 22). Moreover, and here the thought is clearer, law served as a custodian (*paidagōgos* of vv. 24-25) till the coming of Christ, a custodian whose function it was to lead the child to its teacher and to provide any necessary discipline.

This brief and fairly unsatisfying treatment of law is concluded by one of the most profound and joyful passages in the Pauline corpus (vv. 26-29). With this Paul obviously feels at ease. Through faith-baptism we put on Christ to become children of God. "There is neither Jew nor Greek, there is neither slave nor free, there is neither male nor female; for you are all one in Christ Jesus" (3:28). It is this which makes us "Abraham's offspring, heirs according to promise."

This reference to our Christ-position as God's children leads into the following section of 4:1-31. It begins (4:1-7) by contrasting past to present, the period of young adolescence when an heir is not yet in possession of the inheritance to the moment when the full inheritance is an actual fact. This latter happens through the coming of Christ. In him we receive our adoption, and the proof is that God has sent the Spirit of the Son into our hearts. Now — freed from the elemental spirits, the celestial powers controlling the universe — we can pray in the words of Jesus himself, "Abba, Father" (v. 6). We have become, in actual fact, children and heirs.

Since all this is true, Paul wonders in hurt amazement (4:8-11) why these Galatians have moved backwards from the freedom of the children of God to bondage under these mysterious elemental spirits. To placate them, they have entered into religious observances revolving around special "days, and months, and seasons, and years" (v. 10). Such action is slavery, not freedom. Has Paul labored in vain?

What follows in 4:12-20 is a very personal and tender passage. Paul's relationship with these Christians had been so intimate. They would have done anything for him: "You would have plucked out your eyes and given them to me" (v. 15). Why have they now retreated from him and from his teaching? "My little children... I could wish to be present with you now, and to change my tone, for I am perplexed about you" (v. 20).

Paul tries one further appeal, creating an allegory involving the contrasting pictures of Abraham's wives, Sarah and Hagar. To Hagar, the slave woman, was born a child by natural process. Like his mother, he was a slave. To Sarah, the free woman, was also born a child, a freeman, and by means of a promise by God that surpassed the natural process. This, suggests Paul, is somewhat like the present situation of the Galatians. Through God's promise they have become free children of the free woman. Why, then, do they now move backwards into the yoke of the law?

### d) Exhortation (5:1-6:10)

Other commentators believe that the exhortation proper does not begin till 6:1. That may well be, yet chapter 5 —while continuing with the emphasis on freedom that inspired the Sarah/Hagar allegory — concentrates entirely on an exhortation to Christian living.

5:1-15 is a forceful, nuanced and challenging call to Christian freedom. "For freedom Christ has set us free...do not submit again to a yoke of slavery" (5:1). Belief in circumcision as essential, says Paul, is a return to slavery. It involves a necessary dedication to the whole of the law, a belief in justification through observance of law. Paul's good news, Paul's gospel, is quite different. "For in Christ Jesus neither circumcision nor uncircumcision is of any avail, but faith working through love" (5:6). Rarely has Christian theology been reduced to so brief and fitting a formula: faith working through love. From this simple rule of Christian living the Galatians have been seduced. The Galatian dough has been corrupted by a minute but pervasive leaven (v. 9).

It is at this point (vv. 13-15) that Paul nuances his notion of Christian freedom. It is quite the opposite to any form of Christian license. It includes freedom *from*, certainly — and in Romans we shall read of freedom from law and sin and death. But it insists, even more, on freedom *for*. In Christ we have been set free *for* something — so that we "through love (may) be servants of one another. For the whole law is fulfilled in one word, 'You shall love your neighbor as yourself' " (vv. 13-14). With a stunning twist Paul has given Christian freedom a paradoxical and challenging depth. Free we are, free to serve, free to be truly equal, free to be interdependent.

Paul concludes this treatment of Christian freedom (5:16-26) with an insistence on its source, on that which makes it possible. It is the gift of the Spirit, enabling us to resist our natural weakness, the flesh. Led by the Spirit, we are no longer under the law. We turn from the sins to which weakness leads us, the sins — sexual and social abuses — of vv. 19-21, to the works of the Spirit in vv. 22-23. Against these latter there is no law. They are the vital signs of the Spirit's presence, of our own right to pray "Abba-Father," of true Christian freedom. In this domain, law has nothing to say.

6:1-10 is a simple exhortation to gentle fraternal correction (vv. 1-2), to proper humility (vv. 3-5), to gratitude toward teachers of the word (v. 6), to a persistent sowing-in-the-Spirit, a cultivation of the works of the Spirit that yield an eternal harvest. In short, "let us do good to all, and especially to those who are of the household of faith" (v. 10).

### e. Conclusion (6:11-18)

In v. 11 Paul himself takes up the pen — he had been using a secretary — to personalize his letter. And then he attacks his main theme one last time. It is a renewed plea that the Galatians see things correctly. The focus of faith is not circumcision, with law as a necessary consequence, but the cross of Christ. Jesus' death has effected a new creation in which circumcision, or its lack, is meaningless (v. 15). It is the citizens of this creation who are "the Israel of God" (v. 16). Paul concludes with an allusion to his own sufferings (v. 17), the marks of his lashings (2 Cor 11:23-25), perhaps, being contrasted to the unsalvific consequence of circumcision. Paul, who has now had his say and has calmed down to his ordinary tone, wishes to these loved but puzzling Galatians peace and mercy and grace.

## 4. PARTICULAR OBSERVATIONS

### a) Gospel.

The "gospel" of which Paul speaks so frequently in the initial chapters of this letter (1:6, 7[2], 8, 9, 11; 2:2, 5, 7[2], 14) is clearly not the written Gospels of the later evangelists. It is the good news of Christ and his saving work, the good news, especially, that both Gentiles and Jews are called on equal footing to the gift of faith and the Spirit. In Christ, there is neither Jew nor Gentile, but we are equally children of God and heirs according to the promise. Paul's gospel has been beautifully encapsulated by himself in Gal 3:26-29.

### b) Biographical details

This letter gives us important details for establishing a chronology of Paul's life. He tells us that he went up to Jerusalem three years after his conversion (1:18), and then again fourteen years later (2:1). The Greek is constructed in such a way as to make the two figures consecutive, some 17 years in all. Now if we could date this second visit, a simple subtraction of about 17 years would give us the date of Paul's conversion. Dating this second visit of Gal 2 is possible if — as seems more probable — it corresponds to the Jerusalem council described in Acts 15. The argument in favor of such identification notes that in both Gal 2 and Acts 15 the argument is the same — whether Gentile converts are bound to the Mosaic law; the locale is the same — Jerusalem; the decision is the same — freedom for Gentile Christians; the main protagonists are the same — Paul and Barnabas, Peter and James, conservative members of the circumcision party. It is hard to imagine Paul and Barna-

bas meeting twice with Peter and James to discuss the same
point in the same place. The Jerusalem council of Acts 15
can be dated to approximately 49-50 A.D. since it precedes
by a few years Paul's encounter with Gallio in Corinth in
51-52 (Acts 18:12-17). Counting backwards, then, we begin
with the established date of the Gallio encounter (51-52),
move backwards to the Jerusalem council (c. 50) which is
Paul's second visit, then 14 years further to his first trip (c.
36), and a final three years to his conversion (c. 33). This,
of course, places Paul's conversion experience very close to
the actual death and resurrection of Jesus.

The confrontation with Peter in Antioch (Gal 2:11ff)
occurred as these first Christians attempted — not too
successfully — to put theory into practice. It proved easier
to proclaim the freedom of Gentile Christians than it was
to live with the consequences of such a decision. And one
of the consequences was the sharing of food as brothers
and sisters. But could the Jewish Christians tolerate Gentile food? It was probably this practical difficulty that led
to a *later* request by James (Acts 15:19-21, 29) that Gentile
Christians be circumspect in their use of food when eating
with Jewish Christians. Although Acts 15 combines the
main Jerusalem decision of Gentile freedom with James'
request for circumspection, historically the two decisions
were probably separate in time.

## c) Abraham.

It is in this letter insisting on Gentile freedom from the
law that Abraham is presented — for the first time — as
*the* model for believers. The reason for this choice of Abraham rather than Moses is obvious. Whereas Moses was
identified with Jewish law, Abraham preceded law and was
a model of faith. It is of Abraham that Gen 15:6 states,
"And he believed the Lord; and he reckoned it to him as
righteousness" (Gal 3:6). Abraham becomes for Paul the
inspiring and critical model for belief. He *believed*, and so
left his country for lands unknown; he *believed*, and so had
a child of the promise; he *believed*, and so was willing to

offer his son. In his name were the Gentile Christians to be blessed; they would be saved through a faith like his. And in his offspring, the Christ, were they to receive the promised blessings.

### d) *The curse of 3:13.*

It seems significant to me that Paul introduces this somewhat strange theology of the curse removed by Christ who, himself, became in his crucifixion a curse for us. I believe that Paul's interest in the crucifixion as curse statement of Dt 21:22-23 is more than theoretical. *Saul,* the persecutor of early Christianity, may well have believed that Jesus' death on the cross proved that he was accursed by God, and that, as a consequence, faith in Jesus as the messiah, as the Christ, was absolutely blasphemous. Christians, therefore, deserved persecution with death. If so, Paul's subsequent conversion to the risen Lord must have left a residue of the "curse problem" in Paul's mind. Gal 3:13 would be a small indication of this.

### e) *Gal 3:28.*

The immediate context of 3:26-29 is, as we have seen, extremely important. From these few verses, a Christian can amass enough substance to live on for a lifetime. In this latter part of the twentieth century 3:28 has become of special importance. What does it mean to say that "there is neither male nor female; for you are all one *(heis)* in Christ Jesus"? The following reflections may be of some help.

i — The Greek text says that we are all one (heis) in Christ. The number one in Greek is an adjective/pronoun with separate forms for the three genders, i.e. heis, mia, hen. It is significant that Paul has chosen the masculine over the neuter. Rather than become one thing, or even one body (sōma = body is neuter), we have become one person. This, again, puts the emphasis on corporal rather than corporate.

ii — This union with Christ Jesus is effected through faith/baptism, the latter a Christian initiation which —

unlike circumcision — is radically asexual. All human beings are eligible, all become united to Christ in identical fashion and with an identical ceremony.

iii — The daily prayer of a Jewish male thanked God that he had not been born Gentile, slave, or woman. Consciously or unconsciously, Paul has turned this prayer upside down.

iv — Of Gal 3:28's three polarities, Paul addressed with energy only the Jew-Gentile relationship because only that centered for him on something absolutely essential, salvation by faith and not by law. It was not sufficient to say, merely, that the difference between Jew and Gentile was irrelevant in the eyes of God. This truth must be lived out and demonstrated in public life. Peter, in Antioch (Gal 2:11-21) must break bread with the Gentiles. He must believe in this equality and be seen to do so.

v — Yet Paul treated the male/female and slave/free polarities as less essential, less demanding. Why?

One's relationship to God could be lived in *inner* freedom and love both as a woman or as a slave, even though both were subjected states.

Universal custom in Paul's world accepted, and was built on, societal hierarchy.

In the light of the expected parousia, the social status quo as a whole teetered on extinction. It was a lame duck administration. Just hold on a bit and the pain will pass!

One huge problem can be all-consuming for a human being. For Paul it was Jew/Gentile. For this issue he lived ...and died. For Martin Luther King it was slave/free = black/white in the United States. For this he lived...and he died. Neither centered in on the male/female issue. That has been left in our hands.

## f) Gal. 5:12.

This extreme statement which seems to leap from circumcision to castration probably takes its origin from Paul's conscious or subconscious paralleling of Judaizing practices to the ecstatic cult to Cybele, "Great Mother of the Gods" in Asia Minor (*Galatia*) at that time. "She was the great parent of gods and men as well as of the lower orders of creation. Especial emphasis was placed upon her maternity over wild nature. She was called the Mountain Mother; her sanctuaries were almost invariably upon mountains and frequently in caves; lions were her faithful companions. Her especial affinity with wild nature was manifested by the orgiastic character of her worship. Her mythical attendants, the Corybantes, were wild, half-demonic beings. Her priests, *the Galli*, were eunuchs attired in female garb, with long hair fragrant with ointment. Together with priestesses, they celebrated her rites with wild music and dancing until their frenzied excitement found its culmination in self-scourging, self-laceration or exhaustion. *Self-emasculation* sometimes accompanied this delirium of worship on the part of candidates for the priesthood" (Encyc. Britt., 1966, vol 10, under "Great Mother of the Gods," 777-778.)

## Recommended Readings

H. Dieter Betz, *Galatians* (Fortress: Hermeneia, 1979) is a classical commentary written by a world-renowned exegete. It is a necessity for truly scholarly work on this epistle.

F.F. Bruce, *The Epistle to the Galatians* (Eerdmans, 1982) is less academic. Written by an amazingly prolific writer, it has much to say to students of all levels.

P. Ellis, *Seven Pauline Letters* (1982), 173-199 follows the customary format of this author. The text accompanies the commentary which is aimed at an intelligent popular audience.

C. Osiek, *Galatians* (Glazier: NT Message #12, 1980) and J.J. Pilch, *Galatians and Romans* (CBC #6, 1983) have written for a wide popular grouping. Both attempts are successful.

Q. Quesnell, *The Gospel of Christian Freedom* (Herder, 1969) is a popular, lively commentary/paraphrase of Galatians which underscores Paul's revolutionary theology of Christian freedom.

# 8

# Paul's Letter to the Romans

## 1. HISTORICAL BACKGROUND

This richly theological letter, usually so formal as to be rightly termed an epistle, was written to "God's beloved in Rome" (1:7). This indicates the early presence of a Roman church founded, presumably, by Jewish immigrants from Palestine. Aquila and Priscilla, expelled with other Jews from Rome in 49-50 A.D. by emperor Claudius (Acts 18:2), may have been among the first Christians in Rome since there is no indication in either the Acts nor in the Pauline letters that they owed their Christian faith to Paul's preaching. This Roman church was both Jewish (Rom 2:17; 7:1) and Gentile (11:13). Paul does not tell us where he is as he writes the letter, but it fits well into that stage in Paul's life c. 57 A.D. after he has left Ephesus during the III missionary journey and while he plans to move on to Jerusalem with financial "aid for the saints" (15:25). His reference to Macedonia and Achaia in 15:26 makes it most probable that he is writing from Corinth during the three months' stay mentioned in Acts 20:2-3. This surmise is stengthened by the reference in 16:23 to Gaius as host. A man bearing the same name is identified in 1 Cor 1:14 as a Corinthian. Paul writes to the Roman Christians to prepare for his inteded visit to them (1:10-15;

15:23) and with hope of thier assistance for his further journey to Spain (15:24).

## 2. LITERARY BACKGROUND

This is the longest of Paul's letters — which explains why it comes first in the Pauline corpus — containing over 7,000 words. It must have taken a long time to write. (Ricciotti, *Paul, The Apostle*, p. 146 estimates a period of some 98 hours of writing time.)

There are major questions concerning the unity of the letter, and these questions center especially on the doxology of 16:25-27, as well as on the whole of c. 16.

### a) The doxology of 16:25-27.

The content of this doxology is ponderous and overweighted for Paul, and most unusual as a letter ending. Moreover, it has a curious history in the various Pauline manuscripts. It occurs at the end of c. 16 in most of the best manuscripts; at the end of c. 14 in the majority of manuscripts; in both places in some; is omitted entirely in a few; is found at the end of c. 15 in the important P 46 which then continues on with c. 16. It is a floating doxology. The combined difficulties of both content and textual history make it most improbable that these verses came from the hand of Paul. They were probably composed later to provide a conclusion to some shortened version of this letter, a version which, perhaps, had excised cc. 15 and 16. It may be significant that Marcion's expurgated text of Romans did, indeed, end with c. 14.

### b) Chapter 16.

Whereas all scholars agree that c. 16 is a Pauline writing, there is animated discussion as to whether it forms an integral part of the letter to the Romans. Numerous difficulties are noted:

i—15:33 reads like the conclusion to the letter;

ii—16:1-2 can be read as the beginning of an idependent letter of commendation for Phoebe, "a deaconess of the church at Cenchreae";

iii—Prisca and Aquila, greeted in 16:3, were last located in Ephesus, not Rome (Acts 18:18-19, 26; 1 Cor 16:8, 19);

iv—16:5 speaks of Epaenetus, the first convert in *Asia*;

v—C. 16 greets with familiarity 16 men, 11 women and two families. How could Paul have known personally so many people in a church (Rome) which he had never visited?

These acute difficulties have led many commentators to believe that Romans 16 was originally an independent letter commending Phoebe to the church at *Ephesus* where Priscilla and Aquila, Epaenetus and Paul's other friends were to be found. Moreover, the exhortation of 16:17-20 seems to be an unnecessary adjunct to all of Paul's theologizing in Romans 1-15. It fits well, however, in a brief note to the church at Ephesus, and actually resembles Paul's warning to the Ephesian elders in Acts 20:29-30.

Although the case for an independent c. 16 is strong, there is a long list of modern commentators who still argue forcefully in favor of the integrity of Romans' 16 chapters. They note that c. 16 is never found apart from c. 15; that c. 16 is hard to accept as a complete letter; that 15:23 is not the customary Pauline conclusion; that Paul adjoins a long series of greetings, not to churches he knows well — as would be the case with the Ephesian church — but only where he has not visited the church and wishes to name individual friends he knows to create a feeling of intimacy. It is precisely this which Paul does in Col 4:7-17 when writing to a church which Paul has not visited, a church founded by Epaphras (Col 1:7).

The question of c. 16, therefore, remains open. My own position is that Romans 1-15 is the primary content of the letter, to which Paul himself added c. 16 as a personal commendation of Phoebe who is carrying the letter — all 16 chapters — to Rome. It is a Pauline postscript, a simple P.S. If this be true, we can identify Tertius of 16:22 as secretary, not only for c. 16 but for the whole of Romans.

## 3. IMMEDIATE PREPARATION

We will study Romans somewhat after the fashion in which we approached 1 Corinthians, utilizing repeated readings of the letter to follow different outlines or individual suggestions. You are first asked to read Romans against the skeleton outline of section 4 which follows. A second reading can consult the literary format scheme of section 5. After this introductory work is finished, the final section 6 will treat at length some of the main theological issues of this letter, and will challenge you to determine for yourself the Pauline sustenance with which you will nourish your own Christian life.

## 4. SKELETON OUTLINE OF ROMANS

*Introduction (1:1-7).*

A formal, heavily theological presentation of Paul, apostle to the nations.

*Thanksgiving (1:8-17).*

Includes Paul's plan to visit Rome (vv. 10-15), as well as his main theme, equal justification for Jew and Gentile through faith (vv. 16-17).

*Body (1:18-11:36).*

This has a determined order.

| | |
|---|---|
| cc. 1-3 | concentrate on *SIN*. All seems lost. |
| c. 4 | presents ABRAHAM as model of salvific faith. All is not lost. |
| c. 5 | introduces us to the basics; |
| | to GOD'S LOVE which initiates salvation, to the work of RECONCILIATION effected in Jesus who is the SECOND ADAM. |

| | |
|---|---|
| c. 6 | points to salvific initiation, to baptism as sacrament of personal resurrection. |
| c. 7 | considers the Jewish difficulty — and Paul is indeed Jewish. If all this is true, what then of the Law? |
| c. 8 | presents the alternative to law, the dynamism of the Spirit. |
| cc. 9-11 | conclude with a necessary consideration of Israel's relationship to the Gentiles. |

*Exhortation*

| | |
|---|---|
| cc. 12-13 | = charisms, charity, government |
| cc. 14-15 | = questions of legitimate foods, of obligatory days, of Christian edification. |

*Conclusion (15:14-33)*

Paul as liturgist of Jesus in the priestly service of the gospel.
Travel plans.
Collection.

*Post-script (c. 16)*

Phoebe the deaconess and Paul's friends.

# 5. ROMANS ACCORDING TO PAUL'S CUSTOMARY LITERARY FORMAT

## a) Introduction (1:1-7)

This introduction is unusual in both length and heavy theological content. It first presents Paul as servant and apostle, chosen to announce the good news. This good news is presented in brief and poetic form. It concerns God's Son as human descendant of David but as "Son of God in power" by virtue of his resurrection from the dead. (Cf. 1 Cor 15:45 where the resurrected Jesus, the last Adam, has become through resurrection "life-giving spirit".) This is the good news that Paul has been gifted to proclaim "among the nations" (v. 5).

Paul addresses "all God's beloved in Rome" (v. 7) to whom, as always, he extends grace and peace.

### b) Thanksgiving (1:8-17)

As usual, Paul thanks God for the faith of this church. To this he adds the personal note that he intends to visit Rome, thus fulfilling a long-cherished hope. Seemingly it is this plan for a fairly proximate visit which has inspired Paul to write at this time. It is important for him that the Roman church know in advance that he will be coming. The thanksgiving ends by bringing into view the main theological issue of this letter, *justification by faith*. The theology of Galatians will be re-presented, equal salvation for both Jew and Gentile. This is the gospel (v. 16): "He who through faith is righteous shall live" (v. 17) or, as we might be more accustomed to hear this quotation from Habacuc 2:4, "The just man shall live through faith." The greater part of this letter will be an involved commentary on this text.

### c) Body (1:18-11:35)

The body of Romans is a cool and reflective reconsideration of the problem already discussed with abundant heat in Galatians. How do the Gentiles, Paul's beloved Gentiles, fit into God's redemptive plan? What, in particular, is their relationship to the Mosaic and Jewish life style? Paul, who plans an imminent return to Jerusalem (15:25) and who finds every stay in the Jewish — and Jewish Christian —capital a time of stress (15:30-32), is putting together, in mind and on paper, a personal apologia for his treatment of Gentile converts. This is not a "head trip" for Paul. It is, rather, the justification of his ministry and of the Gentile Christians. This letter, as a consequence, though cool and logically constructed, speaks of matters that lie close to

Paul's heart. At times his emotions break through (9:1-5; 10:1) for this is the story of Paul's own life.

—i— Sin (1:18-3:20)

This section accents the negative. Sin holds center stage. 1:18-32 deals with one-half of the world, the Gentiles. Though they had been gifted through nature's evidence with the knowledge of the creator God, they exchanged that knowledge and that God for images of humans or birds or animals or snakes which they worshipped instead (vv. 18-23).

Sin brings its own punishment, further sin. So Paul points out, almost ad nauseam, the sins to which the Gentile world had somewhere, sometime fallen guilty. Paul at this point wants to make an impression. He succeeds. Out rolls a long catalogue of sexual sins (vv. 24-27), to be followed by an equally long list of social misconduct (vv. 28-32). The list seems endless. Paul appears to have captured in writing all the sins in his vocabulary. Such sin-lists were a literary form among moralists of Paul's world. They usually — as here —divided offences into sexual and anti-social vices. Cf. in Paul himself 1 Cor 5:10-11; 2 Cor 12:20-21; Gal 5:19-21; Col 3:5, 8; Eph 5:3-5. Romans' list is so extensive because the epistle is intent on building up a hopeless case.

2:1-3:20 deals mainly with the other half of the world, the Jews. Though the text of 2:1,3 exclaims "O man" (anthrōpe in the sexually inclusive sense), v. 17 identifies the individual as Jewish. Here, too, the insistence is on the negative. "God shows no partiality" (2:11), so judgment will fall equally on those Jews who do what they presume to judge wrong in others. God "will render to every man according to his works" (2:6); punishment for those who do evil "the Jew first and also the Greek" (2:9), reward for those who do good "the Jew first and also the Greek" (2:10).

In truth, there is a basic equality in the divine plan (2:12-16). If one is Gentile, outside of the Mosaic law, that person will be treated as such by God. Gentiles have a law in their hearts, a natural knowledge of right and wrong, and their conduct will be judged accordingly. The Jews, beneficiaries of the Mosaic Law, will be judged by that Law. God is an equal opportunity employer. Paul insists (2:17-29) that Jewish belief must be matched by action. It is useless to preach against theft, adultery, idolatry while practicing these vices. It is blasphemous to boast in the law while breaking it. Circumcision is of value only if a man keeps the requirements to which this initiation dedicates him. But it is equally true that the Gentile who observes God's precepts is circumcised, dedicated to God, in his or her own way. Judaism —and here the older Paul is no longer the Saul of his youth —is not essentially based on anything external. "He is a Jew who is one inwardly, and circumcision is a matter of the heart, spiritual and not literal" (2:29). Though Paul's view of Judaism has radically changed, the word *Jew* is here used with real tenderness. Paul, no less than Saul, remains a Jew to the very end.

This leads, in 3:1-2, to what intends to be an exposition of Jewish benefits. What is the advantage of being Jewish, and what is the value of circumcision (3:1)? The answer begins to take shape: "Jews are entrusted with the oracles of God" (v. 2), the sacred writings. But now Paul is distracted and the subject is not reclaimed till 9:4-5. Back to sin we go. There are a few more things to be dredged up. One is the unfaithfulness of part of the Jewish people, an unfaithfulness that provoked God's judgment. Here is a case of human evil provoking divine good. Is this an argument for consciously doing evil? Paul has been charged with such a doctrine, and he resents the charge (3:8). What he has actually said must be along the line of God's free gift of love being magnified by the unworthiness of its human recipients.

3:9-20 conclude this discussion. Paul has emphasized and reemphasized the sinful context of both Gentile and Jewish living: "I have already charged that all men, both Jews and Gentiles, are under the power of sin" (v. 9). He rests his case with a chain of biblical quotations:

Ps. 14:1-3 speaks of the *universality* of sin (vv. 10-12);

Ps 5:9 speaks of sinful *throats* and *tongues* (v. 13);

Ps 140:3 adds the *lips* (v. 13);

Ps 10:7 refers to *mouths* (v. 14);

Is 59:7-8 to *feet* (vv. 15-17);

Ps 36:1 to *eyes* (v. 18).

Paul's case is closed. Look where you may, consider either the Gentile world or the Jewish, everywhere sin is to be found. A proper means to justification is not evident. "For no human being will be justified in his sight by works of the law since through the law comes knowledge of sin" (3:20).

The accent, I have said, has been on the negative. Paul has done this deliberately to set up a study in contrasts, a theological *chiaroscuro*. Consciously or unconsciously he has adopted the same technique as the remarkable theological author of Genesis 3-11 who dredged up one sin story after another (Adam and Eve, Cain and Abel, the sons of God and the daughters of men, the flood story, the sin of Ham, the tower of Babel) to create the dismal contrast to the brilliant entrance of Abraham and the beginning of salvation in Gen. 12. Romans will presently follow the same sequence.

ii—Salvation in Christ through faith like Abraham's (3:21-4:25).

3:21-32 is a virtual bridge that leads from the negative to the positive. "All have sinned and fall short of the glory of God" (3:23). Of that, Romans has already attempted to convince us. Righteousness, justification do not flow from the law, though the law and the prophets do point to the true justifying principle, "the righteousness of God through faith in Jesus Christ for all who believe" (v. 22). In and through faith are justification, redemption and expiation (vv. 24-25). The just God justifies every individual "who has faith in Jesus" (v. 26). There is, therefore, no ground for boasting since it is by God's gift of faith that we are justified, not by works of the law. With regard to this gift,

Jews and Gentiles are completely equal. The law-free Gentiles are justified because of their faith; the circumcised Jews will also be justified, not out of the law but out of faith. This puts law where it should be — as a pointer and guide to Christ — but not as an essential component of salvation.

Once this short bridge has been crossed, Paul hastens to present father Abraham as model for the salvific process (4:1-25). This whole chapter will be his exegesis of, his *midrash* on, Gen 15:6, "Abraham believed God and it was reckoned to him as righteousness." This citation initiates (v. 3) and concludes the chapter (v. 22), with another reference to it in v. 9. With regard to the Jew-Gentile problem, Gen 15:6 is, for Paul, God's own clear solution. It is *faith* that leads to righteousness.

Abraham, says Paul, was not justified through works which merited due reward but through God's free gift, accepted through belief, a blessing apart from works (4:1-9). And this before circumcision, for Gen 15:6, the account of Abraham's faith, precedes Gen 17:24, the story of his circumcision. This chronological sequence means that Abraham is father of both the non-circumcised and the circumcised, but of both in the same fashion, i.e. if they reduplicate his faith. Again, it was to Abraham's faith, and not to his works, that God's blessing on his descendants was promised. Faith, consequently, is almost the opposite of law, for while the promise comes through faith, it is transgressions that come through law (4:15).

Abraham's faith now becomes more specified, it is faith in "the God . . . who gives life to the dead" (v. 17). Paul is moving at this point into what becomes for him the center of his theological thinking, a vision of God which will have a profound effect on the whole of Paul's thought. For Paul's God, and our God, will be Abraham's God, a God who gives life to the dead; and Paul's faith and our faith will be Abraham's faith, belief in the life-giving God.

The first example of this truth follows immediately in vv. 19-21. Abraham believed that God could and would give life to two dead bodies, his and Sarah's. Both bodies were old, with procreating powers long laid to rest. The Greek text at this point is strong and more to the point than that of the RSV. "He did not weaken in faith when he considered his own body *already absolutely dead* (perf. participle), because he was about a hundred years old or when he considered the *deadness* (nekrōsin) of Sarah's womb" (4:19). It was in this life-giving power of God that Abraham believed, and so he was justified. Justifying faith for us is the same: we are asked to "believe in him that raised from the dead Jesus our Lord" (v. 24). Where *Saul's* God was the God of Abraham, Isaac and Jacob, the God of *Paul* has become more sharply delineated as the God who gives life to the dead, initially to Abraham, primarily to Jesus, and ultimately to all who, possessing Abraham's faith, believe in the risen Lord. For Paul, the process of salvation is, and always has been, the same — faith in the life-giving God. Witness Abraham, witness Jesus, witness ourselves.

—iii— The Elements and Results of Justification (5:1-8:39).

Chapter 5 is given over to a brief presentation of the elements and the effects of the faith-justifying process. Its elements (vv. 1-11) include the deep peace (v. 1) in which Christians rest, the firm hope of sharing in God's own glory (v. 2) and, above all, "God's love...poured into our hearts through the Holy Spirit which has been given to us" (v. 5). This mention of the Holy Spirit is a tiny prelude to the whole of c. 8 in which the Spirit will appear — in contrast to the law of c. 7 — as the dynamism of Christian living. Especially noteworthy at this point in c. 5 is Paul's insistence that the absolute center of Christian life is God's love, God's love for us even as sinners (v. 8). It is this love which has effected our reconciliation (vv. 10-11). It is not that we have reconciled an angry God. Exactly the opposite! A loving God has reconciled us. Romans 5:10-11 is in perfect parallel with 2 Cor 5:18-21.

This leads into a comparison of the two Adams (vv. 12-21). The first Adam was involved in *the reign of sin* (vv. 12-14). Through initial sin did both sin and death become

realities in the world. As all sinned, so all died. Indeed all
died, even though the power of sin operated in differing
fashions. With the first Adam there was command (God's)
followed by transgression (Adam's). A similar process will
be true when the Mosaic law is introduced. But even
between Adam and Moses death remained...as a sign of
sin's ominous presence? as a sign of human weakness even
apart from law?

The reign of sin is opposed by the superior *reign of
God's free gift in Jesus* — a second Adam (vv. 15-21).
These verses are the equivalent to a glorious cry of O Felix
Culpa (O Happy Fault) from the depths of Paul's heart.
His is now a life of freedom, peace, and intense joy in the
Lord. Jesus' saving gifts seem and feel so inspiring that the
reign of sin fades into non-importance. "Much more have
the grace of God and the free gift of grace of that one man
Jesus Christ abounded for the many...Much more will
those who receive the abundance of grace and the free gift
of righteousness reign in life through the one man Jesus
Christ" (vv. 15, 17). If the express commands of law have
the inevitable effect of multiplying transgressions, so, even
more amazingly, does grace now "reign through righteousness to eternal life through Jesus Christ our Lord" (v. 21).
The darkness of cc. 1-3 is being illumined by the bright
realities of cc. 4-5.

6:1-23 is a further reflection on the elements and results
of Christian living. It is initiated by a consideration of
baptism in vv. 1-11. Paul's brief references to this rite in 1
Cor 6:11 and 1 Cor 10:1-2 presented baptism as a washing
and as a kind of "reed sea" union with Jesus. Since then,
Paul's theologizing has reached a new level. Just as baptism by immersion includes the disappearance into the
watery tomb and a reemergence into a cleansed existence,
so does Paul's theology now present baptism as a dying
and rising. "We were buried therefore with him by baptism
into death, so that as Christ was raised from the
dead...we too might walk in newness of life" (6:4). Baptismal union with Christ who died and rose means that we,

too, die and rise. And so, says Paul, "you must also consider yourselves dead to sin and alive to God in Christ Jesus" (v. 11).

Paul's past references to Abraham's God as the God who gives life (4:17), and to justifying faith as belief in God who raised Jesus from the dead (4:24), have prepared for the present doctrine of the death and resurrection of Christians. Through baptism into Christ they encounter Christ who died and rose. In the process, they too die and rise, rise to new life (6:4, 11). This is a present reality, *sacramental* death and resurrection. It also visualizes a future reality, *eschatological* or final death and resurrection (vv. 5, 8).

To the Christian truths of sacramental and eschatological death and resurrection must be added a further element, that of *ethical* death and resurrection, and this Paul does in vv. 12-23. We have been brought "from death to life" (v. 13), from slavery to sin to freedom from it. We who have "been set free from sin have become slaves of righteousness" (v. 8). Sanctification is what we receive, and its end is eternal life (vv. 22-23).

Paul's doctrine on death and resurrection (the paschal mystery) is amazingly rich at this point. He presents to us:

(1) Abraham's life-giving God who gifts us with
(2) Christ who died and rose;
(3) in whom we experience *sacramental* death and resurrection in baptism;
(4) through which we receive assurance of future *eschatological* death and resurrection;
(5) provided that we "yield (our) members to God as instruments of righteousness" (v. 13) through *ethical* death and resurrection.

Paul the theologian is at the top of his form.

If the greater part of these four chapters (5-8) concerns the elements of justification, c. 7, while serving the same purpose, does it by way of denial. Observance of the law is NOT one of the essential elements. This has been a primary truth for Paul's work among the Gentiles, so he must insist upon it once more as he explains what the justifying elements are and *are not*.

Paul begins with a simple comparison (7:1-6), more a technique of personal persuasion than a logical argument. When a husband's death enters into a marriage, the widow is freed from the law of indissolubility. She can marry again. In somewhat similar fashion through the death of Christ we also have died to the law to belong to another, to Jesus himself. Christ's death has been both a dissolving and reuniting factor. Where our sinful nature was prompted by law to bear fruit for death, we are now dedicated to a new life in the Spirit (vv. 5-6).

But, one can object, doesn't this statement, "our sinful passions, aroused by the law" (v. 5), come close to identifying law with sin? This Paul refuses to do. He knows that the law came from God, and so it must be holy, just, good and spiritual (vv. 12-14). Yet, good as it was, it was utilized by sin — conceived almost as a personal power. Law's explicit commands gave the weakness in humanity the opportunity and occasion to fail. "For sin, finding opportunity in the commandment, deceived me and by it killed me" (v. 16).

Paul's language at this point is strong. He speaks in the first person, not as an autobiographical report concerning his own life struggle against sin — Phil 3:6 refutes this — but as a dramatic presentation of the weakness of *pre-Christian* humankind. Even when it ("I") knew what to do, it had terrible difficulty in carrying out its own judgments. Sin seemed bigger than the human person. "For I do not the good I want, but the evil I do not want is what I do" (v. 19). It is sin's crippling use of law that Paul proffers to prove that law is not a saving element. It has, rather, been drafted into the arsenal of sin. In this process sin itself has been revealed in all its nakedness and magnitude (v. 13). Even when God's people (v. 22) delighted in the law, sinfulness kept getting in the way. "Wretched man that I am! Who will deliver me from this body of death?" (v. 24). The answer we already know: "Thanks be to God through

Jesus Christ our Lord" (v. 25a). The chapter concludes with the now anti-climactic summary: without Christ, history has seen the commands of God's law as an ideal, but offenses against it as the actuality (v. 25b).

This has not been an easy chapter to follow. It has not proved easy for Paul to return to his memories of Saul, to the reverence he had for God's law, and then, having justified it, to be able to set it aside rationally for a new kind of life. Paul knows that he, not Saul, is correct, yet he does not yet have clear articulation of the reasons which have led him to his choice. And this, mainly, because it was not reason that led to his conversion but the amazingly unexpected appearance of the risen Lord.

8:1-39 moves the epistle into more comfortable surroundings, into a positive world that Paul knows well through Christian experience, the world of the Spirit conceived of as both an element and a result of justification. This world is the answer to the difficulties of c. 7. "For the law of the Spirit of life in Christ Jesus has set me free from the law of sin and death" (8:2). Where the law of c. 7 provided commands but no inner power to fulfill the commands, finding rather a natural weakness which sin utilized for its own end, the "law of the Spirit of life" (v. 2) provides both counsel and inner dynamism. In Christ, and after his example, we are now spiritually gifted to overcome the weakness of which Paul speaks everytime "flesh" is mentioned. In the Spirit, with the Spirit of God, with the Spirit of Christ we already become truly alive (vv. 9-10), and will eventually be raised as was Jesus (v. 11).

What follows in vv. 12-25 is an urgent call to recognize, appreciate and utilize the adoption as God's children which is the Spirit's gift to us. We, who are led by the Spirit of God, are God's children (v. 14), able to address God as Abba (v. 15), heirs of God and fellow heirs with Christ — though this may, and probably will, entail suffering (vv. 16-17). The pessimistic outlook of c. 7's treatment of law has been completely transformed by this present treatment of Spirit. Saul of the law has become Paul of the Spirit. The text breathes out Paul's feeling of joy at the change.

Vv. 18-25 reach out to include the whole of creation in the newness that Paul feels within himself. Like humankind, creation, too, waits and groans for its renewal. Paul sees a parallel. Just as God has not yet finished working on us and so we still await the complete redemption — glorification—of our bodies, so too the whole of creation still awaits freedom from its bondage to decay (v. 21). Redemption has and will have both a human and a cosmic aspect.

A mellowness flows into the text at this point (vv. 26-39). The Spirit enters even into the natural weakness of our prayers, interceding *with us* through charismatic presence, and interceding *for us* in God's actual presence (vv. 26-27). This gives Paul the assurance that all is right in the world where God's Spirit dwells. God has called us — the "predestined" of v. 29 is not an affirmation of any dogmatic system but of God's undeniable role in our life story — to be the icons of his Son who is, indeed, our older brother (v. 29). And, in so doing, he has both justified us and begun the process of glorification. (Vv 23-25 have already noted that the process is by no means finished.)

This marvelous chapter finishes (vv. 31-39) with a rapturous, poetic, lyric presentation of Paul's view of the God who is love, "If God is for us, who is against us? He who did not spare his own Son but gave him up for us all, will he not also give us all things with him?...For I am sure that neither death, nor life, nor angels, nor principalities, nor things present, nor things to come, nor powers, nor height, nor depth, nor anthing else in all creation, will be able to separate us from the love of God in Christ Jesus our Lord" (vv. 31-32; 38-39). The sharp contrast between chapters seven and eight is complete.

iv—Jew and Gentile in God's Plan (9:1-11:36)

Chapters 9-11 are a distinct unit in Romans, yet they are not independent of the epistle's flow of thought. Chapters 1-3 emphasized sin, c. 4 the justifying faith of Abraham, and cc. 5-8 the elements — positive and negative — of the process of salvation. Spirit has been emphasized over law.

But how does all of this relate to Jewish salvation history, to God's calling the Jewish people into existence and blessing them with their common life and heritage over the centuries? If cc. 1-8 are true, what happens to Judaism and to Israel? The question is extremely difficult today in the twentieth century; it was even more difficult for Paul in the first, for he was personally involved. As a Jewish Christian, what should he say and feel about those in Israel who did not believe as he did, who did not believe that Jesus of Nazareth was the risen Lord? What was he to say about non-Christian friends, relatives, members of his own family? In this section, more than anywhere else in the epistle, Paul's emotional level is high. Some verses are written in tears.

It is noteworthy that these chapters are written as a diatribe, Paul doing a question and answer session with himself. The multiple questions, presumably, are those which Paul has considered personally over the years.

9:1-5 are a powerful statement of Paul's love for his people. Like Moses of old (Ex. 32:32) he is willing to suffer anything — even anathema — for their sake. There follows an excellent enumeration of the blessings of this chosen people, all in the present tense because this people is, and remains, blessed. The list ends with the ambiguous statement at the end of v. 5: "God who is over all be blessed for ever. Amen." This can be the correct translation or, even more in accord with the Greek text, the doxology can be directed to Jesus and read "Christ who is God over all, blessed for ever." Though Paul ordinarily does not *call* Jesus God, he does think of him as such (Phil 2:6, 10; 1 Cor 2:8; 2 Cor 8:9), and in this instance seems to have used of Christ a divine appellation bolder than usual.

The present call of the Gentiles is not an indication of the failure of God's word, but of the freedom of God's choice (9:6-13). As God once chose Isaac, rather than Ishmael, and Jacob rather than Esau, so now God has chosen Gentiles as descendants of Abraham, as *faith-children* of the promise. Citizenship in Israel will be reckoned, not by the relationship of birth but of faith.

Does God's election add up to injustice (9:14)? With this,
Paul enters into an almost impossible knot of problems
(9:14-24). He is certain that nothing escapes God's control.
Therefore if Gentiles believe and Jews don't, God is
involved. But, following this straight-lined mentality, it
must also be that when people do not believe, God is also
involved. But is not God then to blame (9:19)? Paul is caught
in a bind — as all thinkers have been who have attempted to
coordinate God's omnipotence and the presence of evil in
the world. All Paul can do at this point is to proclaim with
certainty and argue from analogy. We are the clay in God's
hands. We have different shapes and purposes, but one
thing is certain: our lives, good or evil, must demonstrate
God's glory and power. In this insistence on God's control,
Paul soft-pedals his own oft repeated belief in human
responsibility. He is certain of both truths: he is not certain
of how they are balanced. It is clearer for him that, de facto,
God has chosen and formed faith-children "not from the
Jews only but also from the Gentiles" (v. 24).

As a good Jew, Paul must be able to find this truth in his
Jewish scriptures. He does (9:25-33) in both Hosea and
Isaiah (vv. 25-28). Hosea's non-people (Gentiles), have
become God's people: Isaiah's remnant represents Jewish
believers. In unexpected fashion, the "non-people" Gentiles
have found the divine process of faith-righteousness, while
the "God-people" Jews, Israel of v. 31, have tripped over a
stumbling block. Pursuing law-justification, they have not
found the justification that comes from faith in the
life-giving God who has raised Jesus from the dead.

Paul stops for a breath at this point, and to raise these
Jewish brothers and sisters of his to the Lord (10:1). Then
he plunges on (10:1-13) into a brilliant resumé of the whole
of his Gospel. Granting Jewish zeal — of which he himself
had once been such an outstanding example — he judges it
misdirected. Its unachieved goal, like the goal of the law
itself, was meant to be Christ: a goal open to all through
faith. Utilizing Dt 30:11-14 as a springboard, he asserts
that righteousness is not far off, not in the inaccessible
heavens (v. 6) or abyss (v. 7), but right at hand. The *good*

*news* is this: "The word is near you, on your lips and in your heart...because if you confess with your lips that Jesus is Lord (Jēsous Kyrios, the original profession of faith) and believe in your heart that God raised him from the dead, you will be saved" (10:9). Here, in one limpid formula, is Paul's whole Gospel, the headline news of Christian faith: JESUS IS RISEN LORD! That is the basic truth, all else is commentary and communal reaction. The beauty of this is that it opens salvation to all. "For there is no distinction between Jew and Greek...everyone who calls upon the name of the Lord will be saved" (10:12-13).

This chapter concludes (10:14-21) with Paul's statement that belief is now possible in practice because, in fact, the good news has been preached everywhere. Paul's vision of the world is limited by the circumscribed geographical knowledge of his day. As he views the scene through the myopic binoculars of the 1st century A.D., the good news has been announced throughout the whole (Mediterranean) world. Indeed, if he can visit Rome and then move on to preach in Spain where land drops into sea, the word will have gone out "to the ends of the world" (v. 18). In this process, Gentile belief and benefits, hopefully, will make Israel jealous (v. 19), more open to God's gift than were their disobedient ancestors at the time of Isaiah 65:2 (v. 21).

Paul tries again (11:1-12) to make sense out of his minimal success in preaching to God's people. Is this a sign of God's rejection (11:1) of the Jews? This Paul cannot believe. There have been many Jewish Christians — he himself among them (v. 1). But, as in the time of the prophet Isaiah, it is the minority, the remnant (v. 5) which has believed. Others have been like those first disciples of Christ chastised in Mark 8:17-21. Having eyes, they see not; having ears, they hear not. Paul shakes head and finger at his contemporaries just as Isaiah did at his (Is 29:10). But this story is not all negative. Israel has not stumbled so as to fall (v. 11). (One would love to have Paul at hand to ask him exactly what this means.) Israel's lack of response has moved Paul and others like him more firmly into the Gentile apostolate. This means riches for the Gentiles. "How much more," says the Jewish Paul, "will their (the Jews) full inclusion mean" (v. 12)!

At this point Paul turns his attention to the Gentiles (11:13-36), eager to remind them firmly of the debt they owe to their Jewish roots. Paul has poured himself into the Gentile ministry, hoping that his fellow Jews would be attracted by the gifts and life of these Gentile converts, hoping that their turning to Christ as Lord would be another instance of Christian resurrection, a turning to "life from the dead" (v. 15). For remember, Paul counsels the Gentiles, that it is the holiness of the original Jewish leaven and of the original Jewish root that sanctifies the Gentile loaf and branches (v. 16).

Paul continues with an analogy (vv. 17-24). As with all analogies it says, "Like this, but also not like this." What comes to Paul's mind is the vision of Israel as a living olive tree, nourished by age-old roots and trunk. Into this tree, to be animated by its life, have been grafted Gentile converts. Their response should not be that of boasting over the Jewish branches (v. 18) pictured as broken off from the tree, but of gratitude for God's kindness (v. 22) and prayer for perseverance. For they, too, can break off (v. 22) — there is clearly no doctrine of predestination here. And so, too, with natural ease can the Jewish branches, through faith, "be grafted back into their own olive tree" (v. 24). This example, of course, limps. It has the positive advantage of presenting Jewish Israel as the root and trunk through which, in which, and by which Christian Israel lives and is nourished. It has the negative aspect of presenting Jewish branches cut off from their natural source of life and history. My own analogy will be presented in the following section with the hope that friend Paul would give it hearty approval. He was hardly the theologian who expected his own to be the last word.

11:25-36 brings Paul's treatment of this difficult subject to an end. As he thinks back over his frequent nonsuccessful encounters with Israel, he sees mostly failure — the biblical "hardening" of v. 25 — which relates in some way to Gentile receptivity. Perhaps that's the clue. In what is an inversion of salvation history up to this point, the Gentiles will enter first (Mk 13:10; Mt 24:14; Lk 21:24) and only then will all Israel be saved (v. 25). They have rejected Paul's good news, yet this has increased the ministry to the Gentiles. Nevertheless, "they are beloved for the sake of their forefathers. For the *gifts and the call of God are irrevocable*" (vv. 28-29). No matter how difficult Paul's relationship with ancient Israel, it remains precious to him and, more importantly, to God. It remains gifted and called, graced and elect. God's future mercy will be the ultimate gift, as it has been for the Gentile believers (vv. 30-32). Paul concludes this long section by placing all in the hands of God. What has happened and what will happen is cloaked in mystery, but somehow God is involved. "O the depths of the riches and wisdom and knowledge of God. How unsearchable are his judgments and how inscrutable his ways" (11:33).

## d) Exhortation (12:1-15:13)

The heavy dogmatic treatment has ended. What remains now is a brief presentation of subjects that Paul could find important in any Christian community, but especially in one like Rome, composed of Jews and Gentiles, living in a highly cosmopolitan area, and under the very eyes of the Roman government.

A brief appeal for chastity comes first (12:1-2), to be followed (12:3-8) by an exhortation for a humble use of the spiritual gifts (charisms) with which we, in the Body of Christ (v. 5) are blessed. Prophecy, communal service, teaching, exhortation, gift giving, acts of mercy are mentioned. To each of us is given one or more of these gifts.

From the charisms, Paul turns to love (as he did in moving from 1 Cor 12 to 13). This passage (12:9-21) is a composition of rare beauty, an ideal of Christian life rarely attained but exceedingly attractive. Only v. 20's "by so doing you will heap burning coals on his head" strikes an unsettling note. Does Paul mean that our loving treatment of an enemy will make him burn with shame? His use here of Prov 25:21-22 is puzzling, but it certainly intends to insist that we are not to be instruments of vengeance. Just recompense is the work of the Lord.

13:1-7 has bothered some advocates of legitimate resistance to oppressive authority. It should not. It is not a law but an ideal. Governance, too, *should* be a gift, a charism. Authorities *should* be God's servants (v. 4) administrating God's justice. And Christians *should* be obedient citizens, willing to pay taxes and revenues, as well as to demonstrate respect and honor. When this ideal picture is shattered by an evil reality, Christians have always made their own the statement of Peter and the apostles, "We must obey God rather than men" (Acts 5:29). As Paul speaks to Roman Christians in the late 50's, he is thinking out of a very dangerous period marked by incipient revolution in Palestine and turmoil in Rome. Don't be a militant zealot, he says. In this Paul, follows the path indicated in both Mk 12:17, "Render to Caesar..." and Mt 26:52, "all who take the sword will perish by the sword." The Christian ideal, for Paul as for his Master, is that of love (vv. 8-10). All the commandments are summed up in this one sentence, "You shall love your neighbor as yourself. Love does no wrong to a neighbor (and that includes authorities); therefore love is the fulfilling of the law" (vv. 10-11).

13:11-14 is Paul's tiny nod to the future parousia, the overpowering preoccupation of his first letter (1 Thess). It still demands some consideration, though by this time in his personal thinking Paul is much more inclined to stress personal union with Christ and his spirit as the primary source of Christian dynamism. Even here it appears, "But put on the Lord Jesus Christ..." (v. 14). This short passage is of immense importance in the history of Christianity. It was through a providential reading of it that Augustine received the courage for his leap into Christian faith. "Take up and read," the voice said. Augustine took up, read, and became a Christian.

14:1-15:6 is a bit of a rerun for those who have studied

the discussion on food in 1 Cor 8-10.

The issues seem evident enough. Is there a distinction to be made between various foods, some to be eaten, some to be avoided (v. 2)? Are there special days of observance (vv. 5-6)? Those whom Paul designates as the "weak" (14:1-2); 15:1) answer yes and act accordingly. The "strong" of 15:1 say no, and suit action to word. The weak are scandalized, the strong are intolerantly amused. Paul prays that the groups can live with a Christian pluralism, acting or not acting out of love for the Lord. "He who observes the day, observes it in honor of the Lord. He also who eats, eats in honor of the Lord, since he gives thanks to God: while he who abstains, abstains in honor of the Lord and gives thanks to God" (14:7). Paul begs for a loving acceptance of different practices, so long as what we do or don't do is intended for the Lord (vv. 8-9). It is the mutual judgment of each other that hurts community (vv. 10, 13). Paul, who in v. 14 sees himself on the side of the "strong," demands that, above all, we walk in love (v. 15). Food and drink and feast days and fast days are all relatively unimportant. What is of primary importance is peace and mutual upbuilding (v. 19). The greater burden here falls on the strong who are called, in love, to avoid all "that makes your brother stumble" (14:21), and "to bear with the failings of the weak...to please (our) neighbor...to edify him" (15:1-2). The strong are not told to refrain from explaining their convictions, but they are told to act with consummate love. And all are called "to live in such harmony with one another, in accord with Christ Jesus, that together you may with one voice glorify the God and Father of our Lord Jesus Christ" (15:5-6).

Paul's discussion of this community issue is hereby finished, but the modern discussion of why this issue has been presented at all continues. Strong voices see here a living issue in the Roman church which is one of the main reasons why Paul has written. Romans was, for them, occasioned by a problem somewhat in the sense that I Cor was occasioned by its accumulation of problems. Equally strong voices believe, rather, that Romans is not at all a

letter reacting to what Paul has heard about Roman difficulties but, rather, a letter written because Paul intends
ultimately to visit Rome and uses the letter to put together
theological reflections of the Jew-Gentile problem as he
prepares for an immediate visit to Jerusalem. The question, therefore, becomes: Does Romans envision Roman
or Jerusalem problems? My own view is that while
Romans 14:1-15:6 is so extended that it must envision a
real Roman problem that Paul has been informed about,
the main content of the letter looks toward Jerusalem and
the still tense Jew-Gentile problem which Paul has only
recently encountered, and been incensed over, in Galatia.
Paul has utilized his project to visit Rome as an occasion to
put his deep theological reflections in literary order.

The exhortation concludes (15:7-13) with a recommendation that we be open to all, that we welcome each other
as Christ has welcomed us (v. 7), whether we belong to the
Jewish half of the world or to the Gentile. Since it is the
welcome to the Gentiles that has come as a surprise, Paul
cites Ps 18:49; Dt 32:43; Ps 117:1 and Is 11:10 as biblical
proof that the open arms extended to the Gentile world
are, indeed, part of God's salvific program.

### e) Conclusion (15:14-33)

The conclusion begins with a description of Paul's
ministry. He has been graced, gifted "to be a minister of
Christ Jesus to the Gentiles in the priestly service of the
Gospel of God" (v. 16). And this he has done. Through the
help of powerful signs and wonders effected by the Holy
Spirit he has helped to spread Christ's good news from
Jerusalem to Illyricum — modern Yugoslavia (v. 19). This
seems to presume a Pauline apostolate even further west
than the sites in Macedonia and Achaia known to us
through Acts and Paul's letters. He has felt called to a
pioneer apostolate, preaching where Christ was still
unheard of. But now Paul hopes to push on further, to visit
Rome and from there to be helped on his way to Spain (vv.
24, 28), the end of the Mediterranean world. First, however,
he must carry the collection to the poor at Jerusalem. By

happy coincidence, Acts 20:4 gives us the names of the representatives of the contributing churches. Acts also tells us that Paul's high hopes regarding the collection were shattered. It did not create a firmer bond between Jewish and Gentile Christians, nor was it seen by the Jewish population as the eschatological advance of the nations to Jerusalem as portrayed in Is 2:2-3 and Micah 4:1-2. Rather, Paul was urged to demonstrate his Judaism, was taken prisoner, almost killed by the mob. Thus he arrived in Rome, not as Christian missionary but as Roman prisoner (Acts 21:17-28:31).

The chapter finishes with a strong petition for prayers (v. 30). Paul always ascends to Jerusalem with anxiety regarding both the Jews and the Jewish Christians (v. 31). He, his ideas and his missionary practices were usually, if not always, an affront to their mentalities. To his fellow Jews, he was a heretic; to the Jewish Christians, he was odd man out, a dangerous innovator. V. 33 reads like an epistolary conclusion though it does not contain all the elements of the customary Pauline ending.

## f) Postscript (16:1-23)

As we have already seen, there is still much discussion concerning the origin of c. 16. My own belief is that it is a P.S., a note to the Roman Christians of commendation of Phoebe the deaconess who is carrying the letter to Rome. It belongs to Romans — from which it has never been found separate — but as a postscript, extremely important in the twentieth century for the unusual view it gives of women's ministry and of Paul's women friends.

This catalogue of Paul's friends mentions — in addition to the collective brethren of v. 14 and the saints of v. 15 —sixteen men, eleven women, and the families of Aristobulus and Narcissus. The number of individuals involved is amazing and, of course, the prime reason for the opinion that this chapter could not have been directed to Rome which Paul had never visited. Even more amazing is the list of women ministers and the praise that Paul heaps upon them.

—i—Phoebe is Paul's Christian sister, a deaconess — the Greek *diakonos* was used for both genders — of Cenchreae, the port city next to Corinth. Besides being termed a *diakonos,* she is also a *prostatis,* a word found only here in the N.T. and translated, with some dispute, as patroness, protectress, or (as in RSV) helper. Paul himself has profited from her assistance (v. 2).

—ii— Prisca, or Priscilla, we have already met. It is difficult to overestimate her importance in the early church. To her and her husband, Paul gives extravagant praise in v. 3. As well he should. They were instrumental in building up the Christian churches in Rome, Corinth and Ephesus. Acts 18:26 credits them with having been the Christian teachers of Apollos.

—iii— Mary of v. 6 is otherwise unknown, but "she has worked hard among you."

—iv— Mention is made in v. 7 of "Andronicus and Junias, my kinsmen and fellow prisoners." They were regarded as a married couple by early Christian exegesis. If, then, Junias was a women — and the name has been found only with female application — v. 7 should read: "Greet Andronicus and Junias, my kinsfolk and fellow prisoners; they are notable among the *apostles,* and were in Christ before me." Paul calls the two apostles. Such early writers as Origen, Jerome and John Chrysostom remarked on the fact that a woman should be called an apostle.

—v— Tryphaena and Tryphosa are termed "workers in the Lord." Persis gets the same commendation (v. 12). .

—vi— The mother of Rufus (v. 13) is unnamed, but she is so dear to Paul that he considers her his mother, too.

—vii— There follows the trio of Julia, the sister of Nereus, and Olympas (v. 15).

There is no other text in the whole of the N.T. literature to match Romans 16 in the accolades it gives to women ministers in the church. Paul, who presents them, does so with obvious love and appreciation. This is the Paul — the real Paul — of Gal 3:28.

The chapter concludes with a short warning concerning dissemination of doctrine contrary to that which they have been taught (16:17-19). There is no hint as to what this doctrine might be. The warning ends with a greeting that looks like the typical Pauline conclusion: "The grace of our Lord Jesus Christ be with you" (v. 20).

A list of greetings follows from men who are with Paul. One has the feeling that they might have dropped in just as Tertius was finishing the final verses, and were added on without much forethought. In rapid fashion appear Timothy, Lucius, Jason, Sosipater, Tertius the secretary, Gaius, Erastus and Quartus. Romans 16 has proved to be a quarry for the names of Paul's friends and fellow workers.

The RSV text, following the lead of the best ancient manuscripts, omits v. 24, "The grace of our Lord Jesus Christ be with you all." There is surely sign of a textual difficulty here. The ending of v. 20, though brief, reads like a Pauline conclusion, except that it's not at the very end of the letter. The omitted v. 24 forms a fitting conclusion, but the ancient manuscripts indicate that it is a later addition by someone who, correctly, could hardly accept v. 23 as a suitable ending. And vv. 25-27, as we have already seen, hardly qualify as a Pauline original. And thus this theological epistle ends with a bit of a question mark. A minor distraction this — the letter itself qualifies as one of the most magnificent expositions of Christian theology ever penned.

# 6. PARTICULAR OBSERVATIONS

Although these notes on Romans have grown larger than originally planned, there is still more to say. What follows is a series of compressed discussions on some points in Romans which seem of exceptional importance to me.

## a) Augustine and Luther

Both of these men, pivotal figures in the history of Christianity, owed their critical choices to the reading of Romans. Augustine received that final impetus toward conversion through a providential reading of Romans 13:11-14. He read it as a direct call from Christ to complete his turn from night to day. He did.

Luther, too, made his critical decision in the light of Romans. In the midst of deep anxiety and sense of guilt, with the feeling that his sinful self was not, and could never become, acceptable to the God of holiness, he read Romans 1:17, "The just man shall live through faith" as the liberating breath of a justifying God. Though he could never be sinless, he could be faith-full. That day a reformer was born.

## b) Justified by faith, judged by works

At first reading it is difficult to exonerate Paul from inconsistency with regard to his statements on free *justification* and merited *judgment*. His belief in the free, unmerited gift of God's justifying love which permits of no human boasting needs little documentation here. It is the main burden of Galatians and Romans and occurs in quintessential form in Phil 3:9, "not having a righteousness of my own, based on law, but that which is through faith in Christ, the righteousness from God that depends on faith."

But, at the same time, Paul's belief in judgment according to works is equally clear. "For he (God) will render to every man according to his works" (Romans 2:6). The teaching is also evident in 2 Cor 5:10, "For we must all appear before the judgment seat of Christ, so that each one may receive good or evil according to what he has done in the body." (And cf. 1 Cor 4:5; 6:9; 8:11; 9:27; 10:12; 11:29; Gal 4:11; 5:6; 6:7-10; Rom 8:13-17; 11:21; 14:15.) How is it possible to reconcile these seemingly opposite beliefs?

Paul visualizes faith-justification as God's free gift. If, and as, we accept this gift of God's love, we receive the

Spirit poured into our hearts (Rom 5:5). Thus, the process of justification. As in-Spirited Christians we stand before God as adopted children, brothers and sisters in Christ. All this is God's work, the sign of God's love, a new creation, God's free gift. At this point, however, Paul believes in human accountability. The presence of the Spirit in us should, and must, exhibit the works of the Spirit, those acts and dispositions which, in Gal 5:22-33, Paul terms "the fruit of the Spirit." Thus, though justification is God's gift, though this basic grace is absolutely free, it is not cheap. The works of the Spirit, the human deeds that flow from the Spirit's presence, are the thermometer by which justification by faith can be measured. Good works are both the effect and the visible sign of the reality of faith-justification. In this sense it is a truth, and not a contradiction, that we are both freely justified by God's grace and also judged by the human works that constitute the outward manifestation of the inner life of faith. Justification comes from God's gift: judgment from what works that gift produces. The characteristic of christian living is "faith working through love" (Gal 5:6).

A quote from J.D. Crossan, *In Parables* (Harper & Row: 1973, 80) is apropos. "The challenge of Jesus and Paul was this: obedience does not lead to God, but God leads one to obedience. The question is not God *or* law, covenant *or* commandment, faith *or* works, but, granting both, in which direction does the arrow fly from one to another?. . . So, according to Jesus and Paul, it was the gift of God's presence that made the good life possible, not the good life that made the reward of God's presence inevitable."

### c) Paul's doctrine of salvation

At this point we arrive at the exact center of Paul's theology regarding the relationship of God and humanity. What difference does Christ make to this relationship, and how explain this Christ-difference to twentieth century people? This is a terribly difficult question for a modern Christian of critical bent. We can talk and pray so easily about salvation and expiation and redemption and reconciliation, but what does it all mean? Does it mean anything? Does our world look and act like a redeemed world, even any small part of it? One recent writer states the difficulty clearly: "What can it mean to say that a crucifixion that took place 2000 years ago representatively expiated our sins and reconciled us with God, with ourselves and with one another?" (G. O'Collins, *America*, Oct 1, 1983, 167). And what, in particular, did Paul mean when he spoke of the salvific process and effects of Christ's death and resurrection? This is one of the most difficult problems in Pauline theology today. All that I can do in these pages is describe the various ways in which Paul speaks of salvation and — as a conclusion — state what I believe that Paul's teaching means for men and women of our own times.

Paul's approach to christology is the Emmanuel approach, Matthew's "God *with us.*" Jesus is not studied theologically in himself, but in *relationship to us.* As Paul views Jesus' death and resurrection, he describes this paschal mystery as it affects human beings. He tries one description, yet another, still another until at least eleven different approaches become evident. (The scriptural references here are illustrative, not exhaustive, of Pauline usage.)

—i— Christ's death is viewed as *expiation* (hilastērion) in Rom 3:25. This figure comes from the cult language of Leviticus 16, a passage which speaks of erasure of guilt through the sprinkling of blood on the mercy seat. Paul intends to say that whatever this Yom Kippur sprinkling accomplished, the shedding of Jesus' blood accomplished even more. Jesus' death was like the expiatory process of Lev 16. Paul's theology uses the models of his own time —expiation is one of them. It occurs only this once, here in Rom 3:25.

—ii— Paul also speaks of Jesus' death as a *sacrifice* (thusia) in 1 Cor 5:7; Eph 5:2. We have, again, cult language. What was Jesus' death, theologically speaking? It resembles a sacrifice. Not the customary sacrifice of the Jewish temple and priesthood, still less a literal sacrifice such as occurred in ancient Aztec Mexico City when some 20,000 prisoners were offered at the temple altar on the occasion of its dedication in 1487. But something like that. Jesus was not literally sacrificed to God upon the altar by the priests of his time, but he did die willingly in obedience to God's will and out of love for the people of his ministry.

—iii— Again, Paul speaks of Jesus' death as our *sanctification* (hagiasmos in I Cor 1:30), as that by which we are set apart, consecrated to God's service. The language is, once more, that of cult. And thus our first three Pauline images, models, analogies all take origin from the cult world which Paul knew.

—iv— A fourth description is that of *liberation* (eleutheria of Gal 5:1, 13). The contextual origin is sociological, the freedom from slavery so essential to the Jewish story of the Exodus. Jesus has accomplished for us what can be described as Christian liberation from sin and self, from law and death.

—v— *Redemption* (exagorasē of Gal 4:5) is yet another attempt to explain the paschal mystery. Jesus' death was like the buying back of slaves for whom a price must be paid to the actual owner. Jesus, in respect to us, accomplished something similar. Here, especially, the analogical nature of the description is apparent. Jesus' death was like a buying back. Better not push the analogy too far. Buying back from whom? From Satan? From God? No, it's simply *like* a buying back, which makes it resemble liberation.

—vi— Another figure comes to Paul's mind; it is that of *reconciliation* (katallagē of 2 Cor 5:17-21; Rom 5:10-11). Here the context of the term concerns personal relationships. Husband and wife should be reconciled after a separation (I Cor 7:11); disputing friends should be reconciled before approaching God's altar (Mt 5:24). When Tyndale first translated this Greek term into English, he divined clearly its basic meaning but found no extant English word that could express it. So he invented one, at-one-ment. That beautiful word, whose meaning has now been lost by its unfortunate conversion into atonement, captured the Greek of Paul's thought perfectly. In Christ, God at-one-d us with God's self and with each other. The force of Tyndale's original expression is still striking.

—vii— A seventh term is the one most commonly used in ordinary language, *salvation* (sotēria of Rom 1:16). Fundamentally it connotes a healing, a restoration to health. It comes from a medical context. Christ has healed the radical sickness of the human race.

—viii— Another commonly used expression, seen as of critical importance by Luther, is *justification* (dikaiosunē of Rom 3:21-28). It has a juridical origin and was used by Paul especially to state the freedom of Gentiles from any essential observance of the law. In God's eyes, the Gentiles through faith stand innocent.

—ix— *New creation* (kainē kitsis of Gal 6:15; 2 Cor 5:17) is a ninth description. It insists on divine activity. God, through Christ the second Adam, has moved humanity from an almost non-entity to new being. "Therefore, if any one is in Christ, he is a new creation; the old has passed away, behold, the new has come" (2 Cor 5:17).

—x— Paul speaks also of christian *adoption* (hiuothesia of Rom 8:15; Gal 4:5) or *rebirth*, of a familial passage from God's simple creation to membership in God's intimate family. It is this which Jesus has accomplished.

—xi— Somewhat similar to cases ix and x, but with a nuance all its own, is a final Pauline description, that of *transformation* (summorphous of 2 Cor 3:18; Rom 9:29). Paul preaches an icon theology. Christians are transformed from one degree to another into living icons of Jesus, himself the perfect icon of the Father.

These are eleven different examples which Paul has culled from different contexts, all "groping words" as one exegete has aptly called them, all attempts by Paul to express the richness of the Christ event. No single one of them, nor all of them together, can describe in its completeness the blessing that Jesus has brought to humanity. Some of these terms may be more expressive, more powerful, to the twentieth century mentality than others. Modern men and women are more open, I believe, to the forceful concepts of liberation, reconciliation, healing, rebirth and transformation than they are to expiation, sacrifice, ransom and justification. Paul, himself, who never ceased to search for new expressions, would undoubtedly be delighted if we could coin meaningful descriptions of our own.

Let me now attempt to systematize Paul's thoughts on this immensely important subject. The composite picture includes his beliefs regarding both *anthropology*, the existing nature of humankind, and *christology*, the nature and function of Christ. There seems to be a logical ordering of concepts within this core of Pauline theology.

(1) Men and women were created to be images of God, divine icons.

(2) This divine imaging was lost, shattered, through sin which led to death and was exaggerated and intensified by law, resulting in a humankind of flesh, of weakness.

(3) Yet salvific faith was never destroyed. It was exemplified in the epic story of Abraham who faithed in a life-giving God, a God who could restore vitality to the almost dead bodies of both himself and of Sarah.

(4) Jesus' life and death were the good news, the gospel, revealing as they did what divine imaging means, i.e., living and dying not for oneself but for others. Jesus is God's perfect icon, a new and perfect Adam. And, as risen Lord, he is life-giving Spirit, pouring God's love and life and energy into those who believe.

(5) Humankind thus passes from darkness into light. It can now see in Christ its own goal, the goal of self-sacrificing service. Not only is the goal recognizable, it is also attainable because through faith, through baptism, through eucharist we are so united to Christ that our lives become his, just as his becomes ours. In Christ, our older brother, we become his Body, his family, brothers and sisters one to another, called both to acknowledge this reality and to live it.

(6) In Christ, God's perfect icon, we, too, become icons, images of Christ. What Adam, God's original image, lost we, in Christ, God's perfect image, have now regained. We are back to where the story started, the circle is complete.

Moreover, the divine image in Christ is much more perfect and dynamic than the divine image in Adam. "O happy fault that merited so great a redeemer!"

It is this process that Paul can refer to with any of the eleven analogical terms described previously. What Christ has accomplished is expiation, sacrifice, sanctification, liberation, redemption, reconciliation, salvation justification, new creation, rebirth and transformation: all that and more. "O the depth of the riches and wisdom and knowledge of God" (Rom 11:33)!

I would put two limitations on the above description. First, it applies only to the anthropological dimension, that dimension which is of pressing significance for us. It says nothing about the cosmic eschatology of Rom 8:19-23; 2 Cor 5:19; Col 1:20. The second limitation is that this description concerns *christian* salvation. Paul's vision is limited by Paul's humanity. As a Christian, he speaks of the Christian process. His theology must not be employed to block out from God's loving mercy the vast millions of non-Christian children of the universal Father.

### d) *The central position of resurrection in Paul's thought.*

Much has already been said about this when discussing Romans 6. What follows, therefore, will be brief and in the form of a skeletal ordering.

—i— Saul became Paul through the appearance of the risen Lord. From that moment, the risen Lord and the doctrine of resurrection became central to his life and theology.

—ii— To Paul, Jewish till death, father Abraham appeared as a remarkable model of faith, a model of what always has been and always will be the salvific process, i.e. faith in God who gives life to the dead. Abraham was justified through faith in God who would vitalize his and Sarah's long-dead creative capabilities.

—iii— The supreme example of God's life-giving power is that of Jesus, the Son whom God raised from the dead into glorified life. Following Abraham's example, we who believe that the life-giving God resurrected Jesus are moved into a spirit-informed, transformed life through *sacramental* resurrection (baptism) which necessarily entails *ethical* resurrection from sin to a life of works of the Spirit. Where this occurs, the future *eschatological* resurrection is assured. Paul's thinking is so resurrection-centered that even when he describes his hopes for the future of his own Jewish family he describes it as "life from the dead" ( Rom 11:15). From conversion till death, Paul was the consummate "resurrection Christian."

### e) Paul's syn-compounds

For those fortunate and hard working enough to be able to read Paul in the original Greek, it is striking to catalogue the expressions he uses, and frequently invents, that are compounded with the preposition *syn*, the Greek equivalent of our English *co* or *con* found in words like co-operate, com-passion, com-miserate. A goodly number of these occur in Romans. These syn-compounds are Paul's attempt to express a concept for which the Greek language was not prepared, the concept of the intense, intimate union between Christ and his Christian followers. They are attempts to spell out in detail Paul's assurance that the life he lived was truly a life that Christ lived in him (Gal 2:20).

The first instance — as I view the chronological order of Paul's letters — occurs in Phil 3:10 where the RSV reads: "that I may know him and the power of his resurrection, and may share his sufferings, *becoming like him in his death*..." The English is attempting to translate the brief Greek phrase, *symmorphizomenos tō thanatō* which resists literal translation. For me it means "sharing his form, (Christ's) with regard to death" and refers to our union in baptism with the Christ who died and rose. The impact of the Greek is almost necessarily lost in any literal translation.

The second instance is that of Phil 3:21. The RSV translates, "who will change our lowly body to be like his glorious body..." The Greek reads "*summorphon to somati tēs doxēs autou,*" and the RSV is adequate, if not absolutely precise. Paul intends to say that Jesus will change the Christian's humble body into one sharing the form of his glorious body. Romans gives us nine other examples. In 6:4 we are co-buried with Christ through baptism. In 6:5-6 we are con-natured with Christ's death and resurrection, co-crucified, we have co-died and will co-live. In 8:17 we become co-heirs if we co-suffer so as to be co-exalted. In 8:29 we co-share the iconship of the divine Son. In the attempt to describe the indescribable, Paul pushed the Greek beyond its limits.

### f) Israel in Paul's theology

—i— The main purpose of this final section in Romans is to consider what Paul has to say about Israel. This question is complicated by the sensitivity which modern Christians should have to any and all comments they make regarding their Jewish brothers and sisters. It is further complicated by the fact that Paul's own thinking is, at times, not a paragon of clarity. Paul's difficulty with a Christian theology of Israel is similar to his difficulty with a Christian theology of law — he was too personally involved in both issues to be able to view them without deep emotion.

—ii— While it is clear that the word *Israel* is part of Paul's sacred vocabulary and that it always carries positive overtones, Paul applies it in two different ways. There is the "Israel of God" (Gal 6:16), the Israel of faith, of Jesus, of resurrection. Of this Israel Paul will say, "For we are the true circumcision, who worship God in spirit, and glory in Christ Jesus and put no confidence in the flesh" (Phil 3:3). And, again, "He is a Jew who is one inwardly, and real circumcision is a matter of the heart, spiritual and not literal" (Rom 2:28-29).

Yet Paul will also use "Israel" to speak of those who kept to the law rather than moving to faith, of "Israel who pursued the righteousness which is based on law" (Rom 9:31). For Paul, therefore, there are two Israels, and this complicates the use of the term. Perhaps this is a blessing, since brilliant clarity is no aid when a situation is, by nature, ambiguous.

—iii— Paul's Israel of God includes the faith-remnant from Jewish Israel plus believing Gentiles. "For there is no distinction between Jew and Greek; the same Lord is Lord of all and bestows his riches upon all who call upon him" (Rom 10:12).

—iv— Historical Judaism, Paul insists, is the holy root. "...remember it is not you that support the root but the root that supports you" (Rom 11:18). The Israel of God is grounded in and nourished by the original Jewish trunk and roots. Paul's logic demands that the Israel of God be not a new Israel but a renewed Israel, an evolved continuation of what was. Yet Paul can also speak of a new creation (Gal 6:15; 2 Cor 5:17). His thought is not completely lucid because he wished to hold two truths, continuity and newness, which are not obviously reconcilable.

This holy root, historical Israel, still remains very special to God in Paul's thought and — perhaps even more — in Paul's heart. "They are Israelites and to them belong the sonship, the glory, the covenants, the giving of the law, the worship, and the promises; to them belong the patriarchs, and of their race, according to the flesh, is the Christ" (Rom 9:4-5). "...as regards election they are beloved for the sake of their forefathers. For the gifts and the call of God are irrevocable" (Rom 11:28-29).

—v— Paul attempts to find some good even in his own lack of success in preaching Christ to his fellow Jews. His failure to convince his own people has pushed him toward the Gentiles who have responded with surprising eagerness. Jewish reluctance has been a source of Gentile entrance. Paul hopes that this great good fortune on the part of the Gentiles will provoke and magnify a spiritual jealousy on the part of the Jews. Paul longs for the day when their acceptance of Jesus will be for them "life from the dead" (Rom 11:15). For they are the holy first fruits, the holy root (Rom 11:16).

—vi— Paul's analogy of the natural olive tree from which Jewish branches have been cut off to be replaced by Christian branches is, may I repeat, an analogy. Every analogy limps; every analogy is necessarily a mixture of "like this" but also "not like this". Paul's example has positive aspects so far a Judaism is concerned for, according to it, Christians live by virtue of Jewish roots and trunk, and the cut-off branches refer to individuals and not to a whole people. But it also has a negative aspect which Paul might well be willing to revise in the light of twenty centuries of Christian living. Where does Paul's analogy leave historical, non-Christian Israel? Is it simply a sociological grouping of cut-off branches? I can't imagine that Paul would agree to this. For then how could we possibly explain and appreciate Judaism's irrevocable "gifts and the call of God" (Rom 11:29)?

As a complement to Paul's tree analogy, with its strengths and weaknesses, I would like to present my own, again with strengths and weaknesses. Mine is a "light" analogy. According to this, the light (revelation and moral guidance) of Jewish Israel moves in a centuries-old beam till it hits a prism (Jesus), at which point the light is both magnified and splintered into all directions and colors. This is originally Jewish light, now diffused, enlarged and refracted through Christ to the Gentile world.

This analogy would leave Judaism as its own continuing light and as the initial and abiding source of Christian light. It would present Christianity as multi-splendored light to the nations, centered from Christ, its living and personal focus point, and forever dependent on its Jewish origin. Christianity would be, in grantedly simplistic terms, what some theologians have called "Judaism for the Gentiles".

—vii— I would like to bring this section, and the commentary on Romans, to an end with a list of statements about Israel which are both true, I believe, and meant to provoke discussion.

— Christians are honorary Jews, though our Jewish brothers and sisters may find this hard to stomach. Our Christian roots are so Jewish that we see ourselves but confusedly if we fail to observe, digest and value our Jewish stock.

— The widespread Jewish "no" to Jesus as Christ was a positive factor in the mission to the Gentiles.

—Jewish continued existence over 1900 years as a scattered people of the book and synagogue has been both a mystery and a miracle.

— Judaism remains a people of God's covenant: "For the gifts and the call of God are irrevocable" (Rom 11:29).

— Israel shall be saved (Rom 11:26).

— Both Jew and Christian have difficulty in acknowledging Jesus' Jewishness.

— The whole of Christian history is based on the faith of *Jews* who accepted Jesus as Messiah and risen Son of God.

— In many ways, the messianic era is not yet an accomplished fact.


## Suggested Readings


There is a long list of commentaries on Romans, generally considered Paul's theological masterpiece. Some that you might want to consider are:

K. Barth, *The Epistle to the Romans* (Oxford Univ. Press, 1933) is justly famous as a pre-World War II manifesto of Pauline theology. In a German world invaded by profound evil, Barth's commentary takes its stance on God's side.

E. Best, *The Letter of Paul to the Romans* (Cambridge Univ. Press, 1967) is directed successfully to an audience without "specialized theological knowledge, and no knowledge of Greek and Hebrew." Best does fine work.

C. H. Dodd, *The Epistle of Paul to the Romans* (London, 1959) is a relatively brief but profound study of this epistle, presented with great simplicity. It is a pleasure to read.

P. Ellis devotes 65 pages of his *Seven Pauline Epistles* (1982), 200-264 to Romans. It is well done.

E. Käsemann, *Commentary on Romans* (Eerdmans, 1980) is erudite and heavy. Only for the academic strong at heart.

E. Maly, *Romans* (Glazier: NT Message #9, 1979) and J.J. Pilch, *Galatians and Romans* (Liturgical Press: CBC #6, 1983) are both directed toward a popular reading audience.

There are two tantalizing articles on the relationship of justification and judgment ("justified by faith - judged by works") that provide most interesting reading:

K.P. Donfried, "Justification and Last Judgment in Paul," Interpretation 30 (April 1976), 140-152, and

R. Pregeant, "Grace and Recompense: Reflections on a Pauline Paradox," Journal of the American Academy of Religion 47 (March 1979), 73-93.

J. Fitzmyer has given us an enriching article on "Reconciliation in Pauline Theology," No Famine in the Land (ed. J. Flanagan and A.W. Robinson: Scholars Press, 1975), 155-177. It contributed mightily to my own presentation of the Pauline analogies of salvation.

S. Lyonnet has written a helpful article on the relationship of freedom and law in "St. Paul: Liberty and Law," in *The Bridge,* Vol IV (ed. J. Oesterreicher: Pantheon, 1962), 229-251.

J. Murphy-O'Connor's *Becoming Human Together* (Glazier, 1983) affords clear insight into Paul's anthropology and Christology. My own presentation is indebted to his.

There is an ever growing list of works on Jewish-Christian relationship. The beginner might try:

D. Harrington, *God's People in Christ* (Fortress, 1980)

J. Pawlikowski, *Christ in the Light of the Christian-Jewish Dialogue* (Paulist, 1982)

K. Stendahl, *Paul Among Jews and Gentiles* (Fortress, 1976)

# 9

# Paul's Letter to Philemon

This brief letter presents special complications because of its obvious relationship to Colossians. This is a complicated point, better treated after a consideration of the letter's content than before. As a consequence, the ordering of this chapter will vary somewhat from that of its predecessors.

## 1. GENERAL BACKGROUND

### a) Authenticity.

Philemon is universally accepted as genuine. If not Paul's, what purpose would this tiny personal letter have served? Who would have been interested in it? How and why would it have entered into a collection of Pauline letters?

### b) Length and oldest tradition.

Phm adds up to only 25 verses and some 420 words. It somewhat exceeds the size of the private letters extant from that period, and, in fact, is more than a private letter, incorporating as it does in vv. 2-3, 25 the members of the church at Philemon's place of residence. Although it is not contained in the oldest Pauline manuscript ($P^{46}$) dating from c. 200 A.D., this absence may well be explained by the strong possibility that P[46] was intended to be a collection of letters addressed "to the churches" rather than to individuals such as Philemon. Tertullian tells us (Adv. Marc. 5:20) that Phm was included in Marcion's canon c. 150 A.D. It is also listed in the Muratorian Canon which many date to as early as the end of the 2nd century or, according to others, as late as the 4th.

### c) Canonization.

The simplest explanation for the acceptance of Phm into the Christian canon is that it was universally acknowledged as written by Paul and, consequently, by the Spirit who guided him. J. Knox and E.J. Goodspeed theorized some 40 years ago that Onesimus, the slave of Philemon, later became Bishop Onesimus of Ephesus, named by Ignatius in his letter to the Ephesians 1:3; 2:1; 6:2 (c. 110 A.D.). Onesimus, according to this theory, was also an initial collector of the Pauline literature. If true, and there is little proof here, it would not be surprising that Onesimus included in the collection the brief letter which had played such an important role in his own personal Christian life-story. A second side to this theory is that Onesimus, devoted disciple to Paul, wrote, in Paul's spirit, the Letter to the Ephesians to serve as an introduction to the Pauline collection. In so doing, he understandably shifted God's impartial judgment on wrong-doing slaves (Col 3:25) to that on wrong-doing masters (Eph 6:9).

## 2. IMMEDIATE PREPARATION

Read Phm aloud at least twice. Listen to the tone of the letter. What does Paul want of Philemon?

# 3. PHILEMON ACCORDING TO PAUL'S CUSTOMARY LITERARY FORMAT

## a) Introduction (vv. 1-3)

Note the soft title, "Paul, *prisoner* for/of Christ Jesus". Paul, prisoner and criminal, writes on behalf of Onesimus, slave and criminal. Although Timothy is mentioned, the letter is very much Paul's alone. Note the frequent appearance of "I", as also of the "Paul" of vv. 9 and 19.

Of Philemon we know nothing more than this brief letter tells us. He is a Christian convert of Paul, master of the slave Onesimus, and — reasoning from Col 4:9, 17 which say that Onesimus and Archippus are Colossians — a member of the Church at Colossae which meets in his house. Apphia and Archippus are identified here only by the titles given them in v. 2. Apphia is a Christian sister; Archippus, Paul's co-soldier. Archippus appears also in Col 4:17, so is a member of the Church at Colossae. There is some scholarly opinion that Philemon and Apphia were married, with Archippus being their son, but Paul's phrasing makes this unlikely. If this were, indeed, a family group, one would expect Paul to finish v. 2 with "and your Church in your (pl.) house." He does not, writing rather, "in your (sing.) house," effectively separating Philemon from the other two.

## b) Thanksgiving (vv. 4-7)

This prepares for the body of the letter by praising Philemon as a man of faith and of love toward Christ and fellow Christians (vv. 5, 7), as a person with a strong sense of Christian fellowship. Not surprisingly, many words found in this thanksgiving will appear later in the body of the letter: "prayers" in vv. 4, 22; "heart" in vv. 7, 12, 20; "refresh" in vv. 7, 20; "brother" in vv. 7, 20; "partnership/partner" in vv. 6, 17; "good/goodness" in vv. 6, 14.

## c-d) Body and Exhortation (combined in vv. 8-22)

i— Paul's request is both subtle and insistent. He does not command but, rather, appeals on behalf of Onesimus whom he is returning to Philemon. Paul insists that the command of love be the basis for Philemon's decision. That Onesimus is a runaway is not expressed, but appears to be the most satisfactory explanation of the situation. Paul appeals as the Christian progenitor of both Onesimus (v. 10) and of Philemon (v. 19). (Had Onesimus heard of Paul in Philemon's house?) In a sense, because he has fathered both into Christian faith, they are his sons, consequently, brothers. Even more, through faith, Onesimus has become Philemon's "beloved brother...in the Lord" (v. 16). Paul requests that Philemon treat Onesimus as such. Onesimus has become "beloved brother" to Philemon just as Philemon himself has become "beloved" to Paul in v. 1. A fair amount of punning occurs in vv. 10-11. In Greek, Onesimus means useful, and the slave Onesimus, once useless (achrestos) to Philemon will now become iminently useful (euchrestos) to both Philemon and Paul. Further, chrestos would have been pronounced at that time just like Christos. Onesimus had been a-Christos, without Christ. He is now eu-Christos, well in Christ.

V. 19 may allude to theft on the part of Onesimus as he fled Colossae. Paul's overall intent, then, is clear. He returns Onesimus, but as his own "very heart" (v. 12), as Philemon's "beloved brother" (v. 17). Here, as in Gal 3:28, Paul lays a theological time bomb. Both texts tend to eliminate the inequality of slavery, to which Gal 3:28 added the further elimination of racial and sexual discrimination.

ii—Philemon's dilemma. What were Philemon's options upon receipt of this letter and of Onesimus? In general, he could treat a returned slave completely at his own discretion. Possibilities, therefore, were numerous.

1 — He could slit Onesimus' throat as suitable punishment and as an example to similarly tempted slaves.

2 — He could take him back, while adjoining some

appropriate punishment such as the loss of an eye, ear, hand, or by administering a public flogging.

3 — He could simply reinstate Onesimus to his former duties.

4 — He could grant him full pardon, his freedom.

5 — He could sell Onesimus to another owner, or give him away.

But what would Paul think of (1) or (2), Paul who suggests that he might be Philemon's house-guest in the future (v. 22)? What would happen to discipline in Philemon's house in case of (3)? And would Paul be satisfied with this? Would not option (4) encourage other slaves (both in Philemon's house and in other families) to seek baptism for the purpose of personal emancipation, thus leading to financial losses on the part of their owners? In the actual sociological circumstances of the first century where slavery was accepted as normal — if not necessary — could Christians have a beloved brother/sister who was their slave? What effect would/should the sharing of Eucharist and the kiss of peace have upon the master-slave relationship?

My own guesstimate is that Paul and Philemon would have settled for the same uneasy compromise as is found in Col 3:5-17 and 3:22-4:1. In the latter verses, Paul does not condemn slavery, but attempts a broad portrayal of how both master and slave can christianize their living situations. In Col 3:5-17, on the other hand, a magnificent presentation is made of how Christians should live in relationship with each other. Perfect practice of these verses should logically lead to the disappearance of slavery but Christians have rarely achieved perfect practice. Probably — think I — Philemon simply forgave (3) Onesimus, intending to have him rejoin Paul as soon as possible. This would be the equivalent of option (5).

Verse 19 may mean that Paul felt so personally involved in this case that he wrote the entire letter by hand. This could have made it the only extant document preserved completely in Paul's handwriting.

Verse 22 could be part of the conclusion or, better, is Paul's final, indirect application of subtle pressure. Philemon may have to respond to Paul face to face. The immenency found in many English translations is not quite so strong in the Greek. The imperative "prepare" is not the punctilear, demanding imperative (the Greek aorist) but the more relaxed present imperative, *hetoimaze*. Its more exact English translation would be something like, "Keep a guest room handy for me, etc."

### e) Conclusion (vv. 23-25)

Just as Paul includes in his introduction "the church in your (sing.) house" (v. 2), so does he postulate a shared letter in his final verse (25): "The grace of the Lord Jesus be with you (pl.)." He intends that Philemon's letter be more than personal, and that the whole community be led to accept even slaves, the lowest of the low, as beloved brothers and sisters in the Lord (v. 16). Vv. 21-25 are, in fact, an interesting combiniation of the singular (Philemon) and the plural (Church). Literally, this section reads: (21) "Confident of your (sing.) obedience, I write to you (sing.), knowing that you (sing.) will do even more than I say. (22) At the same time, prepare (sing.) a guest room for me, for I am hoping through your (pl.) prayers to be granted to you (pl.). (23) Epaphras, my fellow prisoner in Christ Jesus, sends greetings to you (sing.), (24) and so do Mark, Aristarchus, Demas and Luke, my fellow workers. (25) The grace of the Lord Jesus Christ be with your (pl.) spirit."

Vv. 23-24 gives us a list of personages which matches that found in the final chapter of Colossians:

| | |
|---|---|
| Epaphras | = Col 4:12 (Cf. also Col 1:7; Phil 2:25ff; 4:18) |
| Mark and Aristarchus | = Col 4:10 (Cf. for Mk, Acts 12:12, 25; 15:37, 39.) For Aristarchus, cf Acts 27:2.) |
| Demas and Luke | = Col 4:14 (cf. for Demas 2 Tim 4:10) |

Note also how Archippus of Phm 1 appears in Col 4:17. It is this striking parallel of early Christians, plus the appearance of Onesimus himself in Col 4:9, that gives rise to the following consideration.

## 4. RELATIONSHIP OF THE LETTERS TO PHILEMON AND TO THE COLOSSIANS: LOCALE AND DATE OF ORIGIN

The endings of Phm and Col, with their lists of identical characters, especially Onesimus in Col 4:9, bind these two letters together. The simplest explanation of this fact would be that they were written by the same author (Paul), from the same place of captivity, at the same time, and sent via Tychicus accompanied by Onesimus (Col 4:7-9), one to the whole Church at Colossae, the other to Philemon, mainly, but also indirectly to the Church. This "simplest explanation," however, runs into a series of difficulties as scholars consider the facts and attempt to determine a time and place when and where such a double composition was possible. The following options seem to be the best possibilities.

a) Phm and Col were written together during Paul's Roman captivity c. 60-62 A.D. This is the traditional opinion and fits well with Paul's possible presentation of himself in Phm 9 as an "old man" (RSV has "ambassador") and into what appears to be in Col a more lately developed theology both of the Body of which Christ has now become head (compare Col 2:10, 19 to Rom 12:3-8), and of eschatology which in Col seems more "realized-actual" (compare Col 3:1-4 to Rom 6:1-11).

The difficulty with this explanation is that Paul, in the definitely genuine Phm, speaks in v. 22 of an imminent (?) visit to Philemon at Colossae. First of all, a journey from Rome to Colossae (over 1,000 miles) was so distant that imminency seems impossible and exaggerated. Secondly, and of even more importance, Paul, himself, tells us in Rom 15:22-28 that from Rome he intends to go westward to

Spain, just the opposite to an eastward journey to Colossae.

b) As a consequence, many modern authors believe that the most probable opinion is that Phm was written by Paul during a captivity in Ephesus not mentioned by Luke in Acts 19:1-20:1. This certainly makes more possible the short trip (c. 100 miles) from Ephesus to Philemon's home. But it also means that it is difficult to conceive of Col having been composed at the same time since it is more developed than Romans, written from Corinth *after* Paul has left Ephesus. Yet Col purports to be contemporaneous with Phm. These authors, thus, are forced to conclude — with other arguments as well — that Colossians is deutero-Pauline, written by a Pauline disciple who has tied his work not only to Paul's spirit but to a definite Pauline letter, i.e. Phm. Phm, therefore, would have been written from Ephesus c. 56 during a captivity unmentioned in Luke's Acts; Col would have been written after Paul's death by a disciple of the apostle who related it to Phm by including an identical list of personages, including even Onesimus himself (Col 4:9).

c) Others believe that the "imminent" visit to Colossae makes Ephesus the likeliest locale for the composition of Phm and believe, also, that Colossians' theology is not so different from that of Romans as to demand that it be post-Romans. According to this explanation, Phm and Col were written at the same time, during a captivity in Ephesus, by Paul who sent them to Colossae via Tychicus and Onesimus. All of this would predate the writing of Romans and, of course, Paul's Roman captivity.

d) My own opinion

i— The evidence is limited and confusing, so that my own opinion is not nearly so firm and decisive as I would like it to be.

ii— The argument in favor of Phm's composition at Ephesus is fairly strong. The proximity of Ephesus to Colossae would explain both Onesimus's successful journey to Ephesus after leaving the house of Philemon and Paul's hope to visit Philemon in the future.

iii— I feel certain that Col was not written from Ephesus before the composition of Romans in Corinth. Colossians is, rather, on the trajectory of Pauline theology after the composition of the great epistles. Thus I find it impossible to believe that Phm and Col were written by Paul at Ephesus. To say that Phm was written during an Ephesian captivity leads inevitably to the belief that Col is deutero-Pauline and that its author, a Pauline disciple, has consciously tied it to Phm by indicating a case of identical characters in his final chapter.

iv— With some vacillation, and with an openness to further arguments and evidence, I favor the traditional opinion that Phm and Col were written together by Paul during the Roman captivity and thence carried to Colossae by Tychicus (Col 4:7) accompanied by Onesimus (Col 4:9). The clear connection between the two letters has a ring of authenticity, while the major difficulties against this position are not nearly so strong as they might appear to be.

(1) As mentioned previously when discussing Philippians' place of origin, Paul's intention to move westward from Rome to Spain had been fashioned some years earlier in Corinth before the period of captivity in Caesarea and Rome. Need it have remained constant during all this turmoil? It might even have been changed precisely after Epaphras had described to Paul the difficulties at Colossae. Defending a shaky, established church at the prompting of Epaphras, its founder, could have seemed of more immediate importance to Paul than a *possibly* successful missionary trip to Spain.

(2) The note of immediacy which seems to appear in Phm 22 and which is used to argue against Roman composition includes within itself a flaw engendered, surely, from our XX century mentality. It is not that the letter would be mailed and arrive in a matter of days while Paul's arrival would take weeks or months after his release. Letters were carried by hand via whatever means of transportation were available. If, by chance, Paul were released soon after the composition of Phm, he could arrive at Colossae almost as soon as Tychicus and Onesimus. With a bit of good luck on his part and bad on theirs, he could even beat them there. Well might he, then, in his letter ask Philemon to hold a

room ready for him since he might be arriving shortly after Philemon's receipt of the letter.

(3) The free type of Roman house imprisonment described by Luke in Acts 28:16, 30 would be more likely to afford Paul easy contact with Onesimus than any possible type of angry imprisonment imposed on Paul after the riot in Ephesus (Acts 19).

## Recommended Readings

Although this tiny letter has not been the object of many learned commentaries, there are a few studies that recommend themselves.

J.T. Burtchaell, *Philemon's Problem: The Daily Dilemma of the Christian* (1973) is a popular treatment of the problems — both ancient and modern — raised by this brief epistle. My own debt to this book will be obvious to all who read it.

M.A. Getty, *Philippians and Philemon* (Glazier, NT Message #14, 1980), gives a very simple commentary on Philemon which she relates to Philippians, both having been composed in Ephesus.

J.L. Houlden, *Paul's Letters from Prison* (Westminster Press, 1970), 225-232 is a very brief, but solid, treatment of this Pauline note.

E. Lohese *Colossians and Philemon* (Hermeneia: Fortress, 1971) is a genuinely academic commentary. Philemon is an authentically Pauline writing. Colossians, on the contrary, was written, not by Paul, but by a Pauline theologian, a member of a Pauline school, likely based in Ephesus.

# 10

# Paul's Letter to the Colossians

## 1. HISTORICAL BACKGROUND

Colossians takes us some 100 miles east of Ephesus into the heart of Asia Minor where Christianity had set up a missionary triangle of new churches at Colossae, Laodicea and Hierapolis (Col 4:13). The churches were neighbors, Colossae being about 10 miles SE of Laodicea and approximately the same distance S of Hierapolis. All were in the Lycus valley in the territory of Phyrgia. Colossians indicates that Epaphras (Col 1:7; 4:12; Phm 23) had founded the church at Colossae and had, at least, assisted in the work at Laodicea and Hierapolis (Col 4:13). It appears certain that Paul had never visited Colossae (Col 1:4, 9; 2:1), though he may well have promoted Epaphras' work while he, himself, was evengelizing Ephesus (Acts 19). Col affirms that these churches are now being menaced by doctrines challenging the primacy of Jesus. It is to this danger that our present letter responds.

## 2. CONTROVERSY SURROUNDING THIS LETTER

a) The major controversy concerns Paul's relationship to the letter. Did he write it or not? By chance, the

## 2. CONTROVERSY SURROUNDING THIS LETTER

a) The major controversy concerns Paul's relationship to the letter. Did he write it or not? By chance, the recommended readings at the end of this chapter break right down the middle on this question. Three answer, yes: the other three favor composition by a Pauline disciple well versed in the apostle's terminology and theology. That division is very typical of modern scholarship. For every affirmation of Pauline authenticity can be found a denial. Let me present first a resumé of the phenomena which have led commentators to deny that the living Paul stands behind this letter, together with responses by those who favor Pauline authenticity.

—i— There are differences in language and style from those of the other Pauline letters. This is true. One commentator, E. Lohse, *Colossians and Philemon* (Fortress: Hermeneia, 1971) states: "Altogether in Col there are thirty-four hapaxlegomena, words which appear nowhere else in the New Testament writings... There are twenty-eight words which do reappear in the New Testament, but not in the other Pauline letters... There are ten words which Col has in common only with Eph... Finally there are fifteen words used in Col and Eph as well as in the rest of the New Testament, but not in the other Pauline letters" (pp. 85-86).

This is an impressive array of numbers, and constitutes a strong argument against Pauline authorship. It must be recognized, however, that there are explanations for this extraordinary language. For one, the letter makes use of church creedal statements (1:15-20; 2:9-15), perhaps hymns, which Paul himself probably did not compose. The letter and its terminology is also controlled by the adverse doctrines that the author is opposing. In this instance, the dangerous teachings at Colossae are exotic. Little wonder that their exposition and refutation is expressed in language not ordinarily employed by the apostle. Finally, one must allow for an important personal contribution to the actual writing of this letter by Epaphras. Is it even possible to imagine that Paul — supposing him to have been the actual author — would not have worked hand-in-glove with the founder of the Colossian church in composing this letter? Epaphras (Col 4:12) is right there to send along his greetings. These three facts — the use of creedal hymns, the extraordinary doctrine to be combatted, the presence with Paul of the founder of the Colossian church — go a long way toward explaining the different vocabulary and style found in the letter.

ii— A second difficulty for postulating Pauline authorship is a strikingly different presentation of Paul's doctrine of "the body of Christ." In earlier letters (1 Cor 6:15-17; 10:16-17; 12:12-13; Rom 12:4-5) "the body of Christ" is absolutely Christ-centered. To the risen, glorified body of Christ have been joined all Christians by means of faith, baptism (Gal 3:26-28) and eucharist (1 Cor 10:17). United to Christ, we are his members, his Body. All centers on Christ. The "body of Christ" is Jesus' risen body to which we are joined. In Col, however, a change occurs — in fact, a double change. The body of Christ becomes the *Church* (Col 1:18, 24) of which Christ is now *the head* (Col 1:18; 2:10, 19). A change in direction has occurred. Where previously "body of Christ" conjured up directly the image of a body, Christ's risen body, it now points to church, a kind of corporation. And where, previously, Christ himself stood at center, with believing members joined to him, he now stands above. In graphic fashion, we find the following development:

1. The center of Paul's theology is the risen Christ who, as Lord, pours out the Spirit on believers. "The last Adam," says Paul in 1 Cor 15:45, became a life-giving spirit."

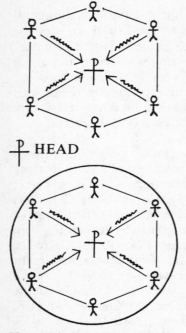

2. To this risen Lord, life-giving Spirit, are united all who believe in faith, die and rise in baptism, and are united sacramentally in eucharist. United to Christ, they also become, of necessity, united mutually in him. This is the image we get from 1 Cor and Rom.

3. In this final picture, that of Col (and Eph), the *centering* Christ has grown smaller, Christ is certainly still there, but, even more visibly, is he *above* the group below which is now "church," almost as though the "church-body of Christ" has been disjointed from the risen, glorified Christ who stands over and above.

Now this is a real difficulty. Can Paul himself have moved his notion of "body of Christ" in such a direction, and what could have caused him to do so? I believe that he could and he did, and that the motivating cause is visible in the letter. All three instances in which Christ is called the head (Col 1:18; 2:10, 19) are found in contexts which speak of the *angels* (1:16; 2:10, 18) and Jesus' supremacy over them. It is the *angel* difficulty, the question in Colossae regarding Jesus' relationship to celestial mediators, which has motivated — almost necessitated — this development. Jesus is over the angels, absolutely superior to them. He is their head. This reasoning has reacted on the "body of Christ" doctrine to move Christ to headship over the Church as well. He remains center, certainly, but just as he has primacy over the angels, so he must have over the faithful of which he is now the head and they the Church. The hint of Christ as "head" in 1 Cor 11:3 has now become an expressed reality. The angel-difficulty has been the motivating cause.

—iii— A third major difficulty is the eschatological (last days) doctrine of Col. Though there is some acknowledgment of a future coming (Col 1:5; 2:17; 3:4, 6, 24), there is more insistence on the vivifying benefits which Jesus has *already* bestowed. God has *already* "transferred us to the kingdom of his beloved Son in whom we have redemption" (1:13-14). We have already received Christ and are to "live in him, rooted and built up in him" (2:6). We "have come to fullness of life in him" (2:10). The Colossians "were buried with him in baptism, in which you were also raised with him through faith in the working of God who raised him from the dead. And you...God made alive together with him" (2:12-13). Raised with Christ (3:1), they should "seek the things that are above, where Christ is, seated at the right hand of God" (3:1). This insistence on the *already* over the awaited *not yet* is striking. Yet it is also a continuation of movement in doctrinal development clearly seen in Romans 6. There, though Paul speaks openly of our *future* resurrection, "For if we have been united with him in a death like his, we shall certainly be united with him in a resurrection like his" (Rom 6:5) and of our *future* life, "But if we have died with Christ, we believe that we shall also live with him" (Rom 6:8), he also takes it for granted that this resurrection to new life has *already* begun. And so he says, "We were buried therefore with him by baptism into death, so that as Christ was raised from the dead by the glory of the Father, we too might walk in newness of life (Rom 6:4). And, "So you also must consider yourselves dead to sin and alive to God in Christ Jesus" (Rom 6:11). What has happened in Col in reference to Rom is that the emphasis has changed. Romans teaches both a future and a present resurrection of Christians to new life. Romans, perhaps, emphasizes the future. I say *perhaps* because the whole glorious chapter eight concentrates on new life in the Spirit. Colossians certainly emphasizes present resurrection to new life, though here, too, affirmation is clearly made of the future: "When Christ who is our life appears, then you also will appear with him in glory" (Col 3:4). Early Paul moved from concentration on future coming in 1-2 Thess to middle Paul with equal emphasis on future coming and present actualization to later Paul with emphatic appreciation of present spiritual benefits.

I conclude that the proposed difficulties to Pauline authorship, though real, are explicable, and that Marcion was correct, as early as 140 AD, when he included Colossians in his catalogue of Paul's letters.

b) A second, but minor, controversy concerns the place of origin. The main options are Ephesus, c. 56-58, or Rome, some four years later. This point has already been discussed when dealing with Philemon. Colossians was written as companion letter to Philemon, while Paul was prisoner in Rome, c. 62 AD, and carried personally from Rome to Colossae by Tychicus (Col 4:7).

## 3. IMMEDIATE PREPARATION

Read and reread this letter aloud. Note the pervasive insistence on our present, actual life of union with Christ. We don't need angelic mediators; we need not wait for the future; God's blessings are available here and now in Christ. Colossians is a letter of comfort and assurance. Note, too, the critique of some kind of angel worship.

## 4. COLOSSIANS ACCORDING TO PAUL'S CUSTOMARY LITERARY FORMAT

### a) *Introduction* (1:1-2)

This introduction is quite ordinary. Paul is together with Timothy. He places soft emphasis on his divinely-willed apostleship since this is important as he addresses a church which he has never visited and to which he must extend corrective advice. The brethren addressed are the saints at Colossae, called by God's choosing, and faithful in their response. To them Paul extends greeting and a prayer for God's grace and the peace that flows from it.

## b) Thanksgiving (1:3-14)

As usual, Paul continues with a warm thanksgiving in which appear both the divine triad (God Father and Lord Jesus Christ of v.3, the Spirit of v.8) and the trinity of virtues (faith, love and hope of vv. 4-5). The thanksgiving — again, as usual — points to the subject matter of the letter proper, the necessity to hold on to the gospel as it had been delivered to them by their missionary founder. Recent influences have not been benign. The Colossians are reminded of the gospel as word of truth which came to them from Epaphras (v.7), a faithful minister to them and a messenger to Paul of their Christian love.

Paul has not known the Colossians personally, yet has heard of them through Epaphras and has unceasingly prayed for them (vv. 9-12). The object of his prayer has been the virtues which they need right now as they confront erroneous teachings: knowledge, wisdom, understanding, a proper Christian life, endurance, patience, and joy.

Vv. 12-14 point backwards and forwards. They conclude the thanksgiving (v.12) and serve as transition to the heavily doctrinal body of the letter. In language that probably reflects an origin in some baptismal context, Paul speaks of a Christian sharing in light, deliverance from darkness, transferral into the kingdom of Christ, redemption, forgiveness of sins. Imperceptibly, we have passed from thanksgiving into doctrine.

## c) Body (1:15-2:23)

With v.15 we are immersed in imposing Christological statements. The short initiatory section (vv. 15-20) is a unit, certainly creedal and probably hymnal as well. It is clearly composed of two parts, the first of which speaks of Jesus' role in creation, the second of which centers on redemption. Though the exact point of division is disputed, it appears that "he is the image... the first-born of all creation; for in him all" of vv. 15-16 is balanced by the "he is the beginning, the first-born from the dead... for in him all" of vv. 18b-19. This would divide the hymn into vv. 15-17 centering clearly on creation, and vv. 18b-20 on redemption. V. 18a, "He is the head of the body, the church" can be considered as a point of union between the two concepts. The Christology presented here is profound and intensely packed. When speaking of creation (vv. 15-17), Paul re-presents his icon theology of Jesus who is the image of God, plus the divine *wisdom* that surfaced originally in 1 Cor 1:24, 30. Jesus is God's image, God's wisdom who, in creation, bespoke God, revealed God to humankind. Just as divine wisdom was with God at the moment of creation (Prov 8:22-31), so now is this wisdom identified as God's divine image, a person far superior to any angelic or human power (v.16). Head of angelic powers, he is also identified as head of his Body, of those joined to him in Church (v.18). He has functioned in creation; he has now functioned once more in re-creation. First-born from the dead (v. 18), filled with the fullness of divinity (cf. 2:9), human and divine, this-worldly and other-worldly, he has been able to reconcile in himself, to at-one in himself, the divine and the human, earth and heaven, creating the peace which is unity by his love offering on the cross. This is powerful Chrisitanity, powerful Christology. In Christ, instrument of creation and of redemption, all is at-oned with God, creator and redeemer.

In vv. 21-23 this reconciliation is applied to the Colossians who, from a Gentile status — estranged and hostile — have now become holy and blameless and irreproachable. So they are and so they will remain if, during the present period of seduction, they continue in the faith, in the gospel preached to them, of which Paul is authoritative minister. Risen Lord to Paul to Epaphras to the Colossian Christians: this is the linkage, forwards and backwards, that must be retained.

Paul remains present from 1:24-2:7. Though not the physical evangelist to Colossae — that was the ministry of Epaphras — Paul has suffered for those disciples, completing "what is lacking in Christ's afflictions for the sake of his body, that is the church" (1:24). What one would give to have Paul present to explain the precise meaning of that verse! It probably presumes, or includes, all of the following elements:

—i— an absolute certainty that Christ's death and resurrection were the sufficient cause of Christian salvation;

—ii— an assurance that Christ's sufferings will be paralleled by Christian sufferings and, especially, by sufferings rising from missionary endeavor;

—iii— a certainty, too, that Christ lives (and suffers?) in him (Gal 2:20). An explanation by way of a quota of suffering, of birth pangs, necessary to initiate the messianic era is probably mistaken here since Col emphasizes the present rather than the future.

Paul's sufferings, Christ's sufferings in Paul, have risen from his ministry, that of manifesting *the mystery* hidden for long ages. The mystery is this, "Christ in you" (1:27). The Christ of history is now revealed in person and in function, and he is revealed "in you" Gentiles. The mystery is God's outreach in love to the Gentiles — it was always known that God loved the Jews — and this in and through Christ. *Christ in us*: is this not the heart of Paul's message, of every announcement of the good news? It is this, it is he, that Paul proclaims in both teaching and warning. It is for this that he toils "striving with all the energy which he mightily inspires within me" (1:29).

2:1-7 continues with the same thought, Paul's energetic concern for all those at Colossae and at Laodicea as well, and for all others like them who have never known Paul personally (2:1). Absent from them physically, but present in the spirit, he prays that they survive their hour of difficulty. He prays for their specific needs: love, understanding and knowledge of God's mystery, good order, firmness of faith. And he prays in their defense, too, "that no one may delude you with beguiling speech" (2:4). Vv. 6-7 are precise and directed to the case at hand: "As therefore you received Christ Jesus the Lord, so live in him, rooted and built up in him and established in the faith, *just as you were taught*, abounding in thanksgiving."

It is only now (2:8-23) that Paul moves into the nitty-gritty, the difficulties which this youthful Christian church is facing. And even though the letter presents some concrete details, it is still difficult to spell out exactly what the doctrine is that Paul opposes. The Colossians, of course, would have had no such difficulty. V. 8 is an overall warning against a certain type of human doctrine (philosophy) which is really human deceit, relating not to Christ but to "the elemental spirits of the universe — the *stoicheia*." This Greek term is ambiguous, referring possibly to the elements of air, fire, water and earth or, more probably, to the angelic powers conceived as directive of stars, planets, the material world. In their place, Paul situates Christ as absolute primate. In him "the whole fullness of the deity dwells bodily" (2:9) and it is in him — not in the angelic powers of which Christ is head (v.10) — that the Colossians have come to "fullness of life" (v.10). Christ, therefore, must be the object of their life and worship. Paul had now moved into a description of our relationship to Christ and to his redemptive work (2:9-15). Again, as in 1:15-20, we have a strong creedal statement, perhaps a primitive hymn, permeated with thoughts of baptism. This need not be a Pauline creation: it may, like 1:15-20, have been a church creation used at the baptismal ceremony or during baptismal instructions, but Paul is happy to utilize it here. In Christ, the Colossians have undergone an initiatory circumcision, a spiritual circumcision, by which they were both "buried with him in baptism" and "also raised with him through faith in the working of God who raised him from the dead" (2:12). This concept is twin to Paul's presentation in Rom 6:1-11, but with the sacramental resurrection proclaimed in clearer terms. The basic concept, however, is identical. From death, they have passed to life with him (v.13). What follows in vv. 13-15 is a depiction, mainly in imagery, of the benefits which Christ's death and resurrection have effected. Sins are forgiven: the legal demands of the Mosaic covenant have been cancelled, nailed like a written document to Christ's cross. Whatever spirit powers or angel powers exist have been disarmed.

Like naked prisoners brought home from a military victory, they have been displayed as defeated objects of a public triumph. Under the arch of Christ they plod in dishonor and disrepute.

As a result, continues Paul in 2:16-23, why are you being tempted by a false asceticism and a false doctrine regarding angels? What is this about food and drink, about annual festivals, monthly new moons and weekly sabbaths (2:16)? Such ascetic practices might be called the passing shadow of things to come, but the real substance — in Greek, the *body* — is Christ's. Now that the body (substance) has come, that earthly body of Christ which became risen body of Christ which has further become member-ingathering body of Christ, all else is shadow. Self-abasement, worship of angels, visions are useless, and worse, if one does not hold fast to Christ the head from whom, and only from whom, the body is nourished and unified and receives its growth (v.19).

Paul completes his argument against Colossian errors (2:20-23) with further references to ascetic practices which have become too important to the Colossians. Why these regulations which seem to acknowledge the power of the spirits, "Do not handle, Do not taste, Do not touch" (v.21)? Paul judges them to be sham practices. They appear to be ascetic wisdom, yet are without value (v.23).

In this section (2:8-23) Paul gives us all the information that he will provide regarding the Colossian deviations. The picture for us, the intended audience, is cloudy. There is a combination of exaggerated regard for angelic powers plus a definite bodily asceticism. It is hard to identify the situation. Probably the Colossians have been presented with a tempting doctrine of angelic powers which rule their lives but which can be controlled by the proper ascetic practices, practices which evidence a Jewish element, as witness the new moon and sabbath of v.16. Against the overwhelming power of these spirits, and contrary to the asceticism which was supposed to placate them, Paul proposes the unique factor of Jesus, image of God, the fullness of the deity, in whom we have died and now live, died expressly to the law and whatever power these spirits may be thought to have. These spirits have been conquered, overwhelmed, led as prisoners in triumphal procession. Though this Colossian mixture is not clearly identifiable, it has some relation to other NT passages. Gal 4:3 speaks of a pre-Christian era in which "we were slaves to the elemental spirits of the universe." Vv. 9-10 of the same chapter ask the Galatians how they can possibly "turn back to the weak and beggarly elemental spirits (stoicheia) whose slaves you want to be once more: You observe days, and months, and seasons and years!" And Heb 1:4-14 produces citation after citation to prove Christ's superiority over the angels. The thought world of Paul's time was nervous and anxious about the control which spirits had over the material world and over human life, in particular. Paul sees this as a mistake: Christ is the answer, the only answer, the all-sufficient answer.

### d) Exhortation (3:1-4:6)

We move now into the exhortation for which 3:1-4 serves as a transitional element. Instead of worrying about "self-abasement and severity to the body" (2:23), we should realize that, in Christ, we have been raised, joined with the risen Lord who now sits at God's right hand. If this is true, our thoughts should be directed where the Lord is, for in baptism we have died and our "life is hid with Christ in God" (3:3). This is surely what modern writers call "realized eschatology — the end times are already here" and with a vengeance. Yet there is still a *not yet*, for Christ is still to appear in a glory which we will share with him (3:4).

3:5-17 should be read with baptism in mind. As there is a baptismal death, so there is an ethical death to vice: as there is a baptismal investiture, so there is an ethical investiture of virtues. First comes the death (3:5-11, with vv. 10-11 as transitional). Die, says Paul, to sin, to the sexual sins of "immorality, impurity, passion, evil desire" (v.5) and to that covetousness, that exaggeration of giving to self, which is idolatry. To these five earthly (v.5) components, Paul adds five more dealing with social life. Die to "anger, wrath, malice, slander and foul talk" (v.8). And do not lie. In baptism we have put off an old nature to adopt a new one which will make us true images of our creator. In this new nature is fashioned a God-willed unity of "Greek and Jew, circumcised and uncircumcised, barbarian, Scythian (the ultimate barbarian), slave, free man, but Christ is all and in all" (3:11). Paul exhorts his hearers to die in baptism, to die to sin, the terrible adversary of human and Christian unity.

As the catechumen removed clothing to enter the baptismal font, and was reclothed in new garments after baptismal death, so the Colossian Christians are exhorted to put on and exhibit virtues of a new life. Again, Paul speaks in units of five: "compassion, kindness, lowliness, meekness, and patience" (v.12), forgiving each other as Christ has forgiven us. Love is the ultimate garment. It will create that peace in unity which should be characteristic of our union in one body. And that should lead to thankfulness, the basic Christian attitude as it should be the primary Christian prayer, expressed in "psalms and hymns and spiritual songs" (v.16). Paul concludes with a ringing summons to a Christian life: "And whatever you do, in word or deed, do everything in the name of the Lord Jesus, giving thanks to God the Father through him" (v.17). Paul's exhortation continues down the ages, just as valid and inspiring for us as it was for the Colossians of Asia Minor.

The exhortation is not yet over. Paul tenders *timely* advice to the various classes of society known to his day (3:18-4:1). It was a society centered on the household and assuredly hierarchical. There were husbands and there were wives, and husbands took precedence. There were parents and children; they, too, in order of rank. And there were masters and slaves in descending order. This was the taken-for-granted world of Paul's time. He does not challenge the structure directly — perhaps because he believed the world so close to its end that structure made little difference in such a lameduck administration, or perhaps because such opposition never even occurred to him. Instead, he asks what is for him the more basic question: How should we live as Christians in the society which is ours? In answer, he speaks of wifely obedience and husbandly love (3:18-19); of filial obedience and parental forebearance (vv. 20-21); of servile obedience that does all as service to the Lord (3:22-24) and of a master's just and fair treatment. In the immediate context of v.17's "...do everything in the name of the Lord Jesus," these mutual demands have a Christian softness to them inspired by a love of the loving God. Yet they hardly satisfy our XX century world, nor need they. They aim at Paul's society and not necessarily at ours. The original question remains the same: "How should we live as Christians in the society which is ours?" But, for us, and largely through Paul's insistence on love and unity, society has changed, and that means that relationships have changed. The strict hierarchical order known to Paul has ceded to a more Christian concept of unity-in-differences intended by him (Gal 3:28). To Paul's original question, and, surely with Paul's approval, we are developing different answers.

For those of us who believe that Paul's letters to Philemon and to the Colossians were companion epistles, the suggestion arises that this husband and wife, parent and child, master and slave material may have been incorporated because of Onesimus' strained relationship with Philemon. If so, Paul is asking Onesimus to see in Philemon the Lord Jesus (3:24). He asks Philemon to treat Onesimus justly and fairly, "knowing that you also have a Master in heaven" (4:1).

Paul finishes his exhortation with two brief notes (4:2-6). He encourages prayer (vv. 2-4), prayer in personal thanksgiving and prayer for the success of Paul's work. Though in prison, he hopes that a door be opened — a prison door followed by missionary access — so that he may clearly speak out "the mystery of Christ" (v.3). Finally, he asks that their conduct toward outsiders be wise, gracious, seasoned with the salt of fitting response (vv.5-6).

### e) Conclusion (4:7-18)

Our final verses are a litany of persons almost identical to that already seen in Phm, especially in Phm 23-24. Tychicus

is new, though he will appear again in Eph 6:21. Beloved
brother, faithful minister, fellow servant (v.7), he carries the
letter and will bear with it personal comments and
encouragement. With him goes Onesimus, Philemon's slave
who, besides being "one of yourselves" is also a "faithful and
beloved brother" (v.9). With this, the whole Colossian
church becomes witness and jury to the response which
Philemon must give with regard to his Christian slave.

Other Christians with Paul send their greetings.
Aristarchus (v.10) is one. He is a fellow prisoner. Acts 20:4
probably refers to him in its listing of those who
accompanied Paul as he carried the collection from the
Gentile churches to Jerusalem. Mark, cousin of Barnabas, is
also present. Uncourageous companion to Paul and
Barnabas on their first missionary journey (Acts 13:13),
center of a bitter dispute between Paul and Barnabas at the
beginning of the second journey (Acts 15:36-40), he is now
present with the apostle. Reconciliation has been effected.
Jesus Justus is mentioned in v.11, his brief and only
appearance in the biblical text. These are Paul's only Jewish
companions at this point (v.11).

But Epaphras is there, a member of the Colossian church
(v.12), one who with Paul prays for the church's maturity.
He has been missionary to the three neighboring churches at
Colossae, Laodicea and Hierapolis. Luke, too, is there as is
Demas. Luke is identified as "the beloved physician" (v.14),
an identification which, down through the centuries, has
been applied to the author of Luke/Acts. Though this issue
is disputed, one can still offer a strong argument that this
traditional identification is correct. In accord with this, the
final "we-section" in Acts 27:1-28:16 places Luke in Rome
during Paul's imprisonment, and in the vicinity of Paul as he
writes Colossians.

Vv. 15-16 refer to Laodicea. Paul sends his greetings to
that church, too, and "to Nympha and the church in her
house" (v.15). This reading refers to a woman and her
house-church. As such, it parallels Nympha to Lydia and
her house-church in Philippi (Acts 16:15, 40) and to Priscilla
and Aquila and their house-church in Rom 16:5. The

feminine reading of v. 15, however, though more probable, is not certain. The verse may speak of "Nymphas and the church in his house," but, in either case, we are reminded strongly of the fact of original house-churches and house eucharists in the Pauline churches. It was probably during such house eucharists that Paul expected his letters, and this letter, to be read (v.16). This procedure aided the Christians to identify Paul's writings as sacred, eventually as canonical. The reference in v.16 to "the letter from Laodicea" is enigmatic. Marcion, c. 140 AD, believed this letter was *Ephesians*, and he may have been correct. Other commentators suggest that the letter to the Laodiceans was written by Epaphras, or that it was a Pauline letter now lost. We remain uncertain. But the request of v. 16 suggests an early custom within the churches of exchanging letters which were considered of authoritative origin and of mutual benefit. Collections of Paul's letters could have begun through this custom.

V.17 illustrates once more the one-side-of-a-dialogue difficulty with Paul's letters. Archippus we have encountered in Phm 2. But exactly who he was is uncertain. Even more uncertain is "the ministry which you have received in the Lord" (4:17). We get the uncomfortable feeling of reading someone else's mail.

Paul's concluding v.18 interjects his own handwriting. He has composed the rest of the letter with the assistance of a secretary. Was it Timothy of 1:1, or Epaphras of 1:7; 4:12-13, or Luke of 4:14? We will never know. But we do know that Paul, prisoner, is "in fetters," and that his heart and love are with these beloved Christians. Grace, God's gift, the whole of God's bounteous and magnificent gift be with them!

## 5. SOME PARTICULAR CONSIDERATIONS

a) Numerous commentators have pointed to the large amount of *baptismal material* contained in Col. One such deposit is 1:12-14. The Father chose us "to share in the inheritance of the saints in light. He has delivered us from the dominion of darkness and transferred us to the kingdom of his beloved Son, in whom we have redemption, the forgiveness of sins." We could easily be listening to a part of the baptismal ceremony proper, or to a bit of an accompanying homily.

2:9-15 also centers on baptism, expecially vv.11-13. Through Christian circumcision, initiation "you were buried with him in baptism, in which you were also raised with him through faith in the working of God who raised him from the dead. And you, who were dead in trespasses and the uncircumcision of the flesh, God made alive together with him, having forgiven us all our trespasses..." Paul's God, who is the life-giving God, has given new life to the risen Christ and new life to Christians now risen through baptism.

3:1-17 sounds just like a baptismal homily. To those who have died (in baptism) and whose life is hidden with Christ in God (v.3), Paul gives advice concerning a required corresponding ethical death and resurrection. "Put to death" (v.5) a perverse way of living. "Put on" (v.12) the opposing virtues, just as the newly baptized put on white garments as they came up out of the font. All that today's preacher need do is change v.11 into modern categories, and this section still functions as a powerful baptismal homily.

It is evident that Paul determined to oppose Colossian errors by reminding these Christians of the baptism in which Christ became center of their lives. No more of those eccentric beliefs about angel worship. Christ, and only Christ, is center and head.

b) Not surprisingly, with Paul's insistence on baptism there is a corresponding appearance of *his "syn" expressions*, those verbs or phrases that couple us intimately with Christ. In 2:12-13, the Colossians were, in baptism, buried with Christ, raised with him and made alive together with him. In 2:20, they died with Christ and in 3:1 were raised with Christ. And, just as their life is hid with Christ (3:3), so they will eventually appear with him in glory (3:4). This usage is very similar to that of Paul in Rom 6, and for the same reason: Paul is speaking of baptism, sacrament of incorporation into the risen Lord. And so, in Rom 6, Paul spoke of being buried with Christ (v.4), of being united with him in death and resurrection (v.5), of being crucified with him (v.6), of both dying with Christ and living with him in v.8. Paul's baptismal theology and, indeed, the whole of Paul's theology places emphatic insistence on this intimate union with the risen Christ by which his life becomes ours. Through baptism and through Christian living we become transformed into him. "I have been crucified with Christ; it is no longer I who live, but Christ who lives in me" (Gal 2:20). This intimate union with the risen Lord has often, and with reason, been called the dynamic center of Pauline theology.

# Recommended Readings

R.E. Brown, *The Churches the Apostles Left Behind* (Paulist, 1984) 47-60 provides a clear analysis of the strengths and weaknesses of the ecclesiology found in Col and Eph, both of which are, for Brown, post-Pauline.

I. Havener, *1 Thessalonians, Philippians, Philemon, 2 Thessalonians, Colossians, Ephesians* (Liturgical Press: CBC #8, 1983) offers a fine exegesis of Colossians, though he has difficulty explaining its purpose as a pseudonymous letter, the position he has adopted.

J.L. Houlden, *Paul's Letters from Prison* (Westminster, 1970) has written a truly excellent commentary, suitable for readers of all levels. He defends the Pauline authenticity, while locating the letter's origin in Ephesus.

L.T. Johnson, *Invitation to the New Testament, Epistles III* (Image Books, 1980), 29-70 is a brief commentary, but much to the point. Paul is the author of Col. Discussion questions are practical for today's living.

E. Lohse, *Colossians and Philemon* (Fortress: Hermeneia, 1971) is the classical, academic treatment. Lohse concludes against Paul's authorship, believing, rather, that the letter was composed by "a theologian schooled in Pauline thought."

P.V. Rogers, *Colossians* (Glazier: N.T. Message #15, 1980) presents the letter as genuine, written by Paul in Rome c. 61 AD. The commentary is well done, written for the ordinary reading public of the twentieth century.

# 11

# Paul's Letter to the Ephesians

## 1. GENERAL INTRODUCTION

Ephesians is different. It is sister to Colossians, in the sense of sharing the same realized eschatology (salvation is now), of defending against spiritual powers on high, of visualizing the Body of Christ as the Church whose head is Christ. And so it shares the same difficulties with regard to postulating Paul as author. In fact, it further exasperates the difficulties by pushing realized eschatology even further (in 2:6 we find ourselves sitting with Christ in the heavenly places), and by emphasizing Christ's fullness, a fullness that appears to demand a cosmic Christ spread throughout the whole universe. These seemingly unPauline characteristics are balanced, on the other hand, by a magnificent development of elements that are truly Pauline. Never before has Paul's doctrine of reconciliation been presented so brilliantly and so simply: it consists in the *unity* of Jew and Gentile (the whole world, consequently) in Christ, and in Christ with the Father. Commentators often speak of Ephesians as the quintessence of Pauline theology, and it is.

We Christians would be vastly poorer without it.

Its language and style are also different. Rather than respond to precise problems — even Col did that — it is basically positive, calmly spelling out its doctrine of unity and peace in a language of prayer and of worship. Paragraph after paragraph lends itself to instant prayer, even today, and parts of it have a ring of liturgy, of worship. Sentences can be long and involved, but always with an elevated tone. We don't exactly read Eph, we pray it. If it lacks the give and take, the thrust and response and nitty-gritty of 1 Cor, it offers, instead, copious material for prayer, for contemplation and meditation, for worship in common. For this commentator, it seems especially fitting as the document with which we shall end our presentation of friend Paul.

## 2. DESTINATION AND AUTHOR

a) Ordinarily the *destination* of Paul's letters is found in the introductory verses. In this instance we are disappointed. Though many of the old manuscripts read, "to the saints in Ephesus," the very best manuscripts lack "in Ephesus" and leave an awkward Greek phrasing which is often translated too smoothly as "to the saints who are also faithful in Christ Jesus." The awkward Greek seems to have something missing, a blank, which makes it possible, if not probable, that the letter was actually a circular epistle meant to be relayed to various churches, of which Ephesus may have been the first. The name of the next church to which it was going would have been written in the blank before it was delivered. The transmission of the text has left us with the two versions: copies of the document as presented to Ephesus and, again, with the document in its undetermined form. A large number of modern commentators, consequently, view Ephesians as this type of general circular letter.

For those who believe that *Paul* wrote this letter for the church at *Ephesus*, there is a further complication. The text, itself, indicates that Paul did not know the addressees personally (1:15; 3:2-3; 4:21). Yet he did know the Ephesians, and very well (Acts 19). The theory of a circular letter circumvents this difficulty. Marcion, Pauline advocate par excellence c. 140 AD, believed that Ephesians was actually the letter to the Laodiceans mentioned in Col 4:16.

b) If the destination of Ephesians is a subject of controversy, even more is *the question of authorship*. As I see it, there are three main opinions.

—i— Paul is the author in the same sense that he authored Gal or Rom or any of his other genuine letters. But he is, of course, older, more experienced, imprisoned, more calm and less energetic.

—ii— The opposite extreme believes that Paul had no living, direct influence on this writing. The epistle was authored, rather, by a disciple who knew Paul's theology and writings extremely well, but who developed that theology even further than its already clear extensions in Col, of which this author made extensive use. Ephesians was thus the first commentary on Col, as well as being a remarkable summation of Pauline theology.

—iii— A third opinion tries to have the best of both worlds. The author of Eph is the imprisoned Paul writing a circular letter to various churches in Asia Minor while under the influence of the theological developments necessitated by the response to Colossae. Paul is no longer the vibrant missionary writing in response to mission problems and opportunities. He is, rather, an elderly man of prayer and worship, gifted through liberal prison circumstances (Acts 28:30-31) with long periods of quiet time during which he composed this theological treatise which is penetrated with prayer passages and multiple echoes of his *stretched* Col theology. In the writing, he has been assisted by a secretary whose individual contributions may have been considerable. Tychicus, as messenger and postman, will carry with him Colossians and Philemon, both intended for Colossae, as well as this third letter meant to be circulated among the churches in Asia Minor. It eventually became known as Ephesians, perhaps because Ephesus is where it started its rounds.

For myself, I walk a narrow line between ii and iii, waiting for further information or argument to move me definitely in either direction. Just as I am ready to affirm Paul as author because of the amazing Pauline characteristic of unconscious digression found in 3:1,14 where the opening thought of 3:1 is broken off, to be resumed only in 3:14, up comes the very unPauline reference to salvation in the past tense in 2:5,8: "by grace you have been saved." For genuine, or younger, Paul, while justification is past, salvation is present or future. Other individual arguments for and against Paul's authorship will appear in the commentary.

## 3. TIME AND PLACE

For those — and they are the majority — who do not believe in Pauline authenticity, almost any place of composition is possible, and any time after Paul's death. Any time, that is, between 70-100. Ignatius of Antioch knows the letter c. 110. For others who believe that Paul was involved in writing this letter, the date would be as late as possible in Paul's life, while he was a prisoner in Rome.

## 4. DIVISION

We have been following the customary Pauline letter five-point division and will continue to do so in the next section. As a valuable memory aid, however, it might be advantageous to note a very simple breakdown of Ephesians. It begins and ends like a epistle. Apart from that it has two main sections, the first dogmatic, the second moral. These two are divided by a doxology. Schematically it looks like this:

## Simple memory division corresponds to Paul's customary format

| | |
|---|---|
| Letter (1:1-2) | a) Introduction (1:1-2) |
| Dogmatic section (1:3-3:19) | b)  Prayer-thanksgiving (1:3-23) |
| Doxology (3:20-21) | c) Body (2:1-3:21) |
| Moral section (4:1-6:20) | d)  Exhortation  (4:1-6:20) |
| Letter (6:21-24) | e)  Conclusion  (6:21-24) |

## 5. EPHESIANS ACCORDING TO PAUL'S CUSTOMARY LITERARY FORMAT

Ephesians resists a tight format. Its various parts flow harmoniously in and out of each other. It differs from Paul's occasioned letters and is — even more than Romans — more of a treatise than a letter proper. In many respects it is a long public prayer of praise placed into the literary form of a letter. Even so, the customary fivefold format is readily identifiable.

### a) Introduction (1:1-2)

This introduction is very similar to that of Col, except that — in the best manuscripts — the "at Ephesus" equivalent to "at Colossae" is missing. Timothy, too, is missing. The letter purports to be Paul's alone.

### b) Prayer and Thanksgiving (1:3-23)

This section is unique, containing not only the customary thanksgiving (vv.15-23) but also the long blessing prayer — what Jews would call a berakah — of vv.3-14. Such a blessing is not unknown in Paul's writings since it can be found also in 2 Cor 1:3ff., but it is unique to have both blessing and thanksgiving placed together as is done here. Unique, too, is the length of the Greek sentences involved. In the Greek, the whole of the prayer (vv.3-14) is one sentence, as is the whole of the thanksgiving (vv.15-23). The RSV has, in the second instance, succeeded admirably in giving a feeling of what the original Greek looked like and felt like.

The opening prayer-berakah of vv. 3-14 is an overture to the whole epistle, announcing clearly the overall theme of unity in Christ: "...destined us in love to be his sons through Jesus Christ...as a plan for the fullness of time, to unite all things in him, things in heaven and things on earth (vv. 5,10). This prayer is a rapturous utterance of awe at the plan of God which has been revealed in Jesus. It is a trinitarian plan, with reference to the Father (vv.3-6) as initiator, to the Son as redeemer (vv. 7-12), and to the Spirit as the initial gift, the down-payment, the guarantee (vv. 13-14). Each division is separated by its concluding phrase, "to the praise of his glory" (vv.6,12,14). It is an eternal plan, "before the foundation of the world" (v.4), inspired by love (vv.5,6,8). And the goal of the plan is unity: we are all called to be children of God in Jesus, the one child (v.5), both *Jews* who first hoped in Christ (v.12) and *Gentiles* (v.13) who, having heard the gospel and believed, have been sealed in baptism by the Holy Spirit, that first payment which guarantees for all believers the inheritance of Israel. As mentioned, this is all one sentence, intensely packed. When read aloud and slowly, it sounds awesome enough to be part of a eucharistic prayer.

The thanksgiving follows (vv.15-23). It is, again, one long, solemn sentence, filled with heavy theological pronouncements. Paul offers thanks for their faith and love and hope (vv. 15,18). He prays that the God and Father of Lord Jesus Christ may grant these Christians wisdom, revelation, knowledge so that their eyes, enlightened in baptism, may see both the richness of the saints' inheritance and the power which works in them. This is the same power that worked in Jesus, that raised him from the dead and placed him at God's right hand (Ps 110:1), far above any spiritual powers that can be named. All things rest under his feet (Ps 8:6) for he is head, universal sovereign, in favor of his Church, the Body of him who fills all things.

In a sense, we've come a long way from the problem solving of 1 Cor, from lawsuits and women's veils and food sacrificed to idols. What we're thus into now is meditation and contemplation. The audience of this letter is asked to prayerfully meditate God's eternal plan. Through faith and love and hope, through baptism, God's power has entered into their lives. Before their eyes is painted this image of the risen and exalted Jesus, head over the angelic powers, head, too, of his personal church, Jesus whose influencing touch extends throughout the universe.

### c) Body (2:1-3:21)

Chapter two is the heart and soul of this epistle, a brilliant theological attempt to spell out the meaning which Jesus has for humankind. Its beginning (2:1-5) might remind us of the movement of Romans, universal sin cedes to God's love. "You (Gentiles) were dead" (2:1) through trespasses and sins. In fact, we were all living lives worthy of wrath and punishment. Echoes of Rom 1-2! But then God, Paul's life-giving God, "out of the great love which he loved us...made us alive together with Christ" (2:4-5). So far, the theology is strictly Paul's. What follows, however, in vv. 5b-10 extends the boundaries. While the recognition of faith and grace as God's gift, not subject to human accomplishment and boasting (vv.8-9), are Paul's constant teaching, the here-and-now benefits of God's grace are magnified. "You have been saved" say both verses 5 and 8. Paul, rather, while speaking of justification as a past event for Christians, customarily refers to salvation as something being accomplished in the present and yet to be consummated in the future (Rom 5:9-10; 1 Cor 1:18). But here, together with present salvation, we find present resurrection and even present exaltation (v.6). God has, indeed, "made us sit with him in the heavenly places in Christ Jesus." *In Christ Jesus* is the operative phrase, and logic is pushed to its limits. If it is true that we are united to

Jesus, and it is true, and if it is true that Jesus sits at the Father's right hand, which he does, then it must also be true that in some way we are all there with him. For the moment, in prayer and contemplation, we have left this world to inhabit God's. We are "his workmanship," (v.10) God's creation, destined to walk in the good works that God has prepared for us. How ideal it sounds in prayer!

2:11-22 pulls us back a bit toward the ground in its magnificent picture of Christ as the peacemaker, as the creator of at-one-ment. The text addresses Gentiles (v.11) primarily, reminding them of their past religious experience. They were the non-circumcised, alienated from Israel and its promised Christ, ignorant of the covenant promises. What hope and what God did they possess? But, now, what an incredible miracle has happened! The wall between Jew and Gentile — and allusion, probably, to the temple wall excluding Gentiles from inner access under penalty of death — has been broken down. In Jesus' flesh, in his death (v.13), the purpose of the law has been accomplished, and Jesus creates in himself one new human being (v.15). Peace is established; the war is over (v.16). Isaiah's poetry is realized: "How beautiful upon the mountains are the feet of him who brings good tidings, who publishes peace" (Is 52:7). Christ is peacemaker and peace-herald to Gentiles who were far off and to Jews who were near (v.17). In and through Christ "we both have access in one Spirit to the Father" (v.18). What an incredibly beautiful and inspiring bit of theology! The reconciliation of v.16 is described in the simplest of terms. Reconciliation is at-one-ment in Christ of Jew and Gentile, of the world's polarities. All of Paul's theology is synthesized and summarized here in the briefest of concepts. Jews and Gentiles at-oned in Christ, and in Christ with God. Salvation, reconciliation, justification, expiation, whatever Pauline analogy you choose, is defined in the same one word, "Unity." God's plan, God's goal, Christ's life and death and resurrection, all aim at the same purpose, unity. What builds unity — in marriage, in family, in nation, in the world — is God's work and God's design: what disrupts, injures, destroys, frustrates unity is demonic, is sin. The concept is so simple, so profound, so eminently Paul's. If, indeed, Ephesians is the quintessence of Pauline theology, these few verses are the heart both of Ephesians and of all Christian theology.

What follows in vv. 19-22 is a joyful catalogue of Gentile blessings. In Christ, they have become fellow citizens of God's kingdom, members of God's household. This household is like a building with the Christian apostles and prophets as its foundation, with Christ as its cornerstone. Living Body becomes living building. This one grows into a holy temple, a dwelling place — in the Lord, of course — for "God in the Spirit" (v.22).

One concludes the reading of 2:11-22 with awe. If this is not Paul, it is a Pauline disciple who has surpassed his master. The language has been moving, the basic concept deep and powerful and, yet, so simple. Christian life and Christian challenge have been proposed in such concise terms. At-one-ment in Christ, and in Christ with God. That is what we are, and that is what we are about. Christ offers it to us by his example: Christ offers it to us by the power of his Spirit. In Christ, through Christ, for Christ, we are sent to at-one the world.

Attention is now turned to Paul himself (3:1-19). With the doctrine of reconciliation still bright in our memories, the text continues, "*For this reason*, I Paul, a prisoner for Christ Jesus on behalf of you Gentiles..." but it doesn't end. A long disgression follows through vv. 2-13 before we finally get back to where we started with v. 14's repetition, "*For this reason I* bow my knees before the Father..." This digression is a Pauline fingerprint, so typical of Paul (cf. Rom 3:1-2, completed only in Rom 9:4-5) that it is a forceful, if not quite apodictic, proof of his authorship. It is hard to imagine a disciple who has so imbided his master's style as to do such an unconscious imitation, or, again, a disciple who consciously takes time and effort to separate the content of v.14 from its beginning in v.1 so as to trap us into a mistaken identity. The digression, itself, speaks of Paul's great grace, his summons to preach to the Gentiles "the mystery" (vv.3-4), the long hidden and now recently revealed truth that the Gentiles have been called, that they "are fellow heirs, members of the same body, and partakers of the promise through the gospel" (v.6). For our author, the mysteries of God unravel into one core revelation: the Gentiles are called, called into union with the Jews in Christ, in God. This is *the mystery*, the good news, of which Paul has been made minister or servant (v.7). Paul's grace, Paul's gift has been the call to preach this to all humanity so that God's gracious wisdom might be manifested to all, even to heavenly powers, whoever and what ever they might be. With reference back to 2:18, we hear of the bold and confident *access* we have to God in Christ (3:12). Paul's sufferings, therefore, are not a sign of defeat but, rather, are *for us*, in our behalf. An echo sounds of Col 1:24.

3:14 takes up v.1 after this long digression. "For this reason," because of this glorious summons to unity in Christ, Paul worships the Father with bent knees, praying that we be strengthened through the Spirit, that Christ may dwell in our hearts through faith, that we may comprehend the breadth and length and height and depth of God's love, so as to be filled with that enormity of God that fills the whole universe. In v.18's "breadth and length and height and depth" some interpreters have seen a cosmic cross that touches all ends of the universe. Horizontally it reaches out to the polarities of Jews and Gentile: vertically it touches the polarities of God and humankind. At the cross-point, where all becomes one, is the body of Christ, given by God for human beings, given back to God by Christ, uniting in itself Jews and Gentiles who share one faith, one baptism, one Eucharist.

```
                God
                 |
  Jew ———————    ϼ    ——— Gentile
                 |
              Humanity
```

The body of the letter now concludes with a doxology, a prayer for the praise and glory of God who in all things, and

204 Paul's Letter to the Ephesians

especially in this work of loving reconciliation, "is able to do far more abundantly than all we ask or think" (v.20). To him be the glory for ever and ever. Amen (v.21). This dogmatic section finishes, as it should, in prayer, for it has been composed throughout in meditation and contemplation. Our author, in a sense justified by 3:14, has written it on his knees.

### d) Exhortation (4:1-6:20)

The second half of this letter is exhortation, though dogmatic underpinnings are visible throughout. We are exhorted to lead lives worthy of the calling described in the preceding chapters. This means lives of humility, meekness, patience, forbearance, love, unity and peace (4:1-3). What follows in vv. 4-6 is a magnificent ecumenical creed, one that all Christians can profess and pray and work for. Wherever Christians are gathered, no matter what divergencies have arisen among them over the centuries, all can join hands and — as brothers and sisters in Christ — profess the same essential belief: "There is one body and one Spirit, just as we are called to the one hope, one Lord, one faith, one baptism, one God and Father of us all who is above all and through all and in all." In Paul's theology we are baptized, not into different churches, but into the one body, Christ's risen and glorified body, which unites us together into his Body, the Church. We are baptized, not into church disunity, but into Body unity.

Through this unity into Christ, "grace was given to each of us" (v.7). With a peculiar, personal reading of Ps 68:18, a picture is given us of Christ who has touched all of creation, from its lowest depths to its highest peaks, filling the universe with his presence, and enriching us all with his various gifts. Apostles have been called, as well as prophets, evangelists, pastors, and teachers. These are the heavily ministerial gifts, all "for the work of ministry, for building up the body of Christ" (v.12). The gifts are like Christ himself, for others. They are meant to unite us in faith, to increase our knowledge of the Son of God, to make us grow into mature Christians, indeed, into the mature Christ (v.13). The hope is that our weakness be strengthened, "that we may no longer be children tossed to and fro and carried about with every wind of doctrine" (v.14). We are not told what strange doctrines are being carried about on the winds at this time, but it will be a rare day when some fallacy does not attack the desired unity of Christ's Body. Rather, we should live the truth in love (v.15). The RSV's "speaking the truth" is too curtailing. *Living the truth* is much closer to the Greek original and much closer to the Christian goal. The text continues with another urgent call to Christian maturity, to a growing up into Christ who, as head, gives nourishment and guidance. From him and in him are we joined and knit together, a growing entity that builds itself up in love.

What follows from 4:17 on, till the conclusion in 6:21-24, reads like a homily delivered on the occasion of a baptismal ceremony. Note the *put off* and *put away* of vv. 22,25, as well as the *put on* of v. 24. Just as the newly baptized put off their old clothes for their descent into the waters, and were reapparelled in new white garments immediately afterwards, so Christians will now be told to divest themselves of the works of death and darkness to walk in life and light. Baptismal death and resurrection leads to ethical death and resurrection. This theology is strictly Pauline.

4:17-22 gives the negative. This is where these Gentile Christians once lived — in darkness, alienation, ignorance, licentiousness. But that is not Christ: it is the old man, corrupt, lustful, a shade of the old Adam. In its place we are to "put on the new man" (v.24), the new Adam, truly created in God's image, truly God's living and perfect icon.

There follows a list of small and detailed observations of what life should be for those who "are members of one another" (4:25). No lying; severely controlled anger; no theft but, rather, honest work so we can give to others; no evil talk, but words of edification, for we have been sealed at baptism with the Spirit; no acts of anger and malice, but acts of kindness. As God has forgiven us, so we are to forgive others (4:32). This is the Our Father prayed backwards. 5:1-2 sounds like a summary and conclusion, though it will be followed by further exhortatory remarks. It is hard to beat as a thumb-nail sketch of Christian living: "Therefore be imitators of God, as beloved children. And walk in love, as Christ loved us and gave himself up for us...". This is one of those great Pauline one-liners, a pressure packed description, in the fewest words possible, of what our life is all about.

5:3-5 are a double cut at "immorality and all impurity or covetousness," the abstract nouns decried in v.3 and the adjective/pronouns in v.5. The passage demands that unfitting, silly talk be replaced by thanksgiving. Paul is strong on thanksgiving as the constant, due response of creation to its creator. Vv. 6-14 read like a section from a Qumran Dead Sea community document, with repetitious contrast between the opposing sides of light and darkness. Starting with v.6 we encounter "sons of disobedience...darkness ...light in the Lord ...children of light...works of darkness...light...light...and Christ shall give you light." This language is typical not only of the Dead Sea documents, but also of John's Gospel. It is unknown to Paul's other letters, though its closest counterpart in 2 Cor 6:14 is a passage of uncertain origin. But the idea here in Ephesians is clear, almost too clear. There is a world of light and a world of darkness: the former is inhabited by the children of light, the later by the sons of disobedience. V.14 is almost universally identified as a baptismal hymn, indicating how we pass, in baptism, from sleep and death into the light of Christ. The concept of baptism as an illumination is also shared with the IV Gospel. Certainly the man born blind in John 9 is a model of Christians who pass from darkness to illumination by washing in the pool of Siloam which means *sent* which word, in John, is virtually Jesus' nickname. As we wash in the pool which is Christ, we — blind from birth — begin to see.

Vv. 15-20 are words of encouragement to be wise, truly wise, which means understanding "what the will of the Lord is" (v.17). In what would be a pun in English (but not in Greek), we are told to hold back on the spirits, but be inebriated with the Spirit. Then in vv.19-20 we hear a favorite Pauline refrain: "always and for everything giving thanks" in "psalms, hymns and spiritual songs...making melody to the Lord with all your heart." Paul would feel thoroughly at home on the stage with a vigorous black chorus.

5:21-6:9 is an expanded rerun of the "household rules" (Luther called them that — Haustafeln in German — and the name has stuck in academic circles) which we have already seen and commented on when treating Col 3:18-4:1. What we had to say there about the timely and timeless aspects of these admonitions holds here for their Ephesian equivalents.

All three sections — husbands and wives, parents and children, masters and slaves — have expansions here in comparison to their Col parallels. The advice to children and parents (6:1-4) includes now the reward (v.3) promised in Deut 5:16, and the fathers are asked to provide true Christian education for their children. Though the words to masters and slaves (6:5-9) are almost the same as in Col 3:22-4:1, Ephesians adds on a final challenge to the masters by noting that "there is no partiality with him," with the Lord. Both slave and master will stand together before an impartial judge.

But the main expansion concerns the husband-wife admonition. The core of Col 3:18-19 has been retained, but thoroughly theologized. If Paul has authored both Col and Eph, he has had enough time between the two to rethink the relationship of husband and wife and bring to the surface its sacramental/sign nature. Husband and wife, their love and union and mutual sacrifice, are a sign of Christ and his Church/bride and their love and union and mutual sacrifice. The husband's position of authority in the first century would resemble Jesus' position of authority. From these presuppositions, all else flows. As the Church is subject to Christ, so is the wife to her husband (vv.22-24). And as Christ loved the Church and died for her, "gave himself up for her," so do the remaining verses (25-31) insist on the husband's love for his wife who becomes one body with him. Vv.26-27 detour for just a moment to highlight the sacred birth moment of baptism when the Church, union and personification of all Christians, emerges from the font "without spot or wrinkle...holy and without blemish" (v.27). Christ and his bride, husband and wife, "This is a great mystery" (v.32). The Greek *mysterion* was early translated into Latin as *sacramentum*, making it easy and even inevitable to fit marriage into a Christian sacramental theology. Loving union of husband and wife is visible sign of loving union between Christ and his Church. Sign also becomes challenge — challenge in first century terms to the man in particular, for it is he who is called to love his wife with a love akin to Christ's overwhelming sacrificial giving.

What we have here in 5:22-33 is *incarnate* theology. By incarnate I mean theology rendered in human terms, in the wording, and subject to the sociology, of the first century's strict hierarchical order of society. If this magnificent theology had been authored in our own twentieth century, it would surely have been issued in language adapted to this present period in which reciprocity is more valued than hierarchy, in which interdependence is more virtuous than dependence. With apology to Paul, I suggest that what he would write now, in our age, would resemble the following:

> Be open to one another out of reverence for Christ: wives responsive to their husbands, husbands responsive to their wives, just as the Church should be responsive to Christ, her head and savior. As the Church is responsive to Christ, so should wives and husbands be to each other in all things. Husbands and wives, love each other as Christ loved the Church and gave himself up for her, that he might sanctify her, having cleansed her by the washing of water with the word, that the Church might be presented before him in splendor, without spot or wrinkle or any such thing, that she might be holy and without blemish. Even so, husbands and wives should love each other as they love themselves. For married partners that love each other love themselves. No one ever hates one's own flesh but nourishes and cherishes it, as Christ does the Church because we are members of his body. For this

reason man and woman shall leave father and mother
and be joined together, and the two shall become one.
This is a great mystery, and I take it to mean Christ and
the Church. However, let each of you love each other as
one's self, each open to the other's needs.

One final exhortation remains (6:10-20). It teems with
analogies, military metaphors deriving from the prophecy
of Isaiah. It speaks, too, out of a first century mentality that
equates evil and the demonic with invisible and superhuman
spirits. We contend, not against mere flesh and blood (v.12),
merely human evil, but against more perverse and
pervading powers, "against the principalities, against the
powers, against the world rulers of this present darkness,
against the spiritual hosts of wickedness in the heavenly
places" (v.12). The language echoes Col, as it also echoes
Gal 4:8-9. Against such demonic power, we are
admonished, twice, to put on "the whole armor of God"
(vv.11,13). Isaian metaphors flow in abundance: "having
girded your loins with truth" (v.14) comes from Is 11:5;
"breastplate of righteousness" is Is 59:17; "having shod your
feet with the equipment of the gospel of peace," Is 52:7;
"helmet of salvation," Is 59:17; and "the sword of the Spirit
which is the word of God," a seeming combination of Is 11:4
and 49:2. The advised armor, consequently, consists of
truth, righteousness, the gospel of peace, faith, salvation
and the word of God. To this mighty armament is added
prayer and more prayer (vv.18-20); prayer for perseverance,
prayer of supplication, prayer in particularly that Paul,
God's ambassador in chains, be enabled to speak out boldly
the mystery of the gospel.

## E) Conclusion (6:21-24)

Eph concludes, as did Col, with a reference to Tychicus
who, in the event that both letters are Paul's, will be
postman for Col, Eph and Philemon. Not only does
Tychicus appear in both Eph 6:21 and Col 4:7, what is said

about him in Col 4:8 is now found in exactly the same words in Eph 6:22. For some commentators this is indicative of a non-Pauline writer copying in Eph what Paul — or another disciple — had written in Colossians. For others, like myself, such purported copying bespeaks a mechanical copyist much less endowed with creative genius than the author of Eph. It seems easier to imagine the identical statements about Tychicus as made in similar letters, written at the same period, and to be actually carried by him to neighboring localities. As the passage stands in Eph, Tychicus is meant to be both mailman and messenger. He "will tell you everything...that you may know how we are, and that he may encourage your hearts" (vv.21-22).

This amazing and encouraging epistle concludes with a final prayer for "peace," for "love with faith" (Gal 5:6). Then, with a unique twist for a Pauline composition, it asks that "Grace be with you all who love our Lord Jesus Christ with love unending" (v.24). And with this beautiful thought the Paul of the ten letters disappears from view. But his words, his thoughts, and his prayers have been captured in ink unending, to become our joy, our challenge, and the measuring rod of our faith, our love, our hope, our life.

## 6. SOME PARTICULAR CONSIDERATIONS

a) The theology of *church* is a clear and primary interest in Eph. It takes various forms and is illustrated by various terms and analogies, reducible to three "B's."
i— The Church is the *Body* of Christ, composed of all — both Jew and Gentile — who are united to Christ. This subject is constantly to the fore, appearing in every chapter except the last (1:22-23; 2:15-16; 3:6; 4:4,12,15-16,25; 5:23,30).
ii— The Church is also a *building*. The metaphorical language here virtually bursts its bounds since, if one describes the union of Christians with Christ as building, this must at the same time be a living entity. And so "the whole structure is joined together and grows into a holy temple in the Lord;

in whom you also are built into it for a dwelling place of God in the Spirit" (2:21-22).

iii— The Church is, finally, *bride*, bride of Christ. The figurative language of the Jewish Scriptures, according to which Yahweh was faithful groom to Israel, his bride, has been transferred to Christ who becomes redeeming groom of the Church. His love and self-sacrifice for this spotless bride is the model given to husbands called to an equivalent love and devotion (5:25-31).

b) As was true of Col also, Eph is replete with *baptismal* material. Solving the question of why this is so might be a positive step toward a definite affirmation or negation of Paul's authorship. As we proceed through Eph, the following are certain or probable allusions to baptism:

i— 1:3-14. This berakah which has a strong Trinitarian structure (Father in vv.3-6, Son in vv.7-12, Spirit in vv.13-14, each section finishing with "unto the praise of his glory") seems designed for worship. The conclusion, "*sealed* with the promised Holy Spirit" (v.13) appears to be baptismal.

ii— Three phrases in cc.1 and 2 are probably related to baptism: "...the eyes of your heart enlightened" (1:18); "...made us alive together with Christ" (2:5); "For we are his workmanship, created in Christ Jesus" (2:10).

iii— Is 4:4-6 a baptismal creed? "There is one body and one Spirit, just as you were called to the one hope that belongs to your call, one Lord, one faith, one baptism, one God and Father of us all, who is above all and through all and in all."

iv— 4:22-5:2 could be a baptismal instruction centering on the moral life expected of the new Christian. Note in particular: "*Put off* your old nature...and *be renewed*...and *put on* the new nature...*putting away* falsehood" (vv.22- 25).

"And do not grieve the Holy Spirit of God, in whom you were sealed..." (v.30).

"...forgiving one another as God in Christ forgave you" (v.32).

v— 5:13-14 may refer to the catechumen's confession of sins which thus become visible and, consequently, light, followed by a baptismal hymn: "Awake, O sleeper, and arise from the dead, and Christ shall give light."

vi— 5:26 certainly refers to baptism: "...that he (Christ) might sanctify her having cleansed her by the washing of water with the word."

vii— The whole of 6:10-18 may be a baptismal exhortation.

All of this makes one wonder just how this letter originated and what purpose it was intended to serve. We may have here an origin and purpose completely different from that of the other letters in the Pauline corpus. Its style is solemn, liturgical, hieratic. If Paul is in some genuine way its author, it is the Paul of prayer (not of dialogue, discussion and dispute) that we are viewing.

c) Eph gives us another collection of *syn* (co) compounds. 2:5-6 gives us three in a row as "God who is rich in mercy, out of the great love with which he loved us, even when we were dead through our trespasses made us alive together with (*synezōopoisēsen*) Christ...and raised us up with (*synēgeiren*) him, and made us sit with (*synekathisen*) him in the heavenly places..."

There are other *syn* words, too, but this time emphasizing, not the union we have with Christ, but the union we have in Christ *with each other*. In Christ, we become fellow members. And so we are told in 2:19 that we are "fellow citizens (*sympolitai*) with the saints." In 3:6 the Gentiles become "fellow heirs (*synklēronoma*), members of the same body (*syssōma*), and partakers (*symmetocha*) of the promise in Christ Jesus..." Syssōma, especially, is hard to translate. "Members of the same body" is decent, but the Greek is even tighter and more demanding. It says, literally, "co-body." In Christ we Christians are co-body, the one shared body. Ephesians' theology is finally explicitated in the direct phrasing of 4:25, "...for we are members of one another."

d) Finally, the shape of the Church as it has been known to us down the centuries begins to take definite shape. Eph provides the following elements:

i— *foundation of apostles and prophets* (2:20; 3:5). To them are added (4:11) evangelists, pastors and teachers. They are to build up the Body of Christ and provide assurance of

ii— *unity of faith and knowledge*, in opposition to "every

wind of doctrine" (4:14). This unity includes a simple but ample

iii— *creed*, "There is one body and one Spirit, just as you were called in one hope that belongs to your call, one Lord, one faith, one baptism, one God and Father of us all, who is above all and through all and in all" (4:4-6). This creed may well have been related to

iv— *baptism* which appears clearly in the hymnic fragment of 5:14 and in the passage on christian marriage (5:26-27). The hymnic fragment, as we have seen, is only one of a whole series of verses that agrue for close relationship to the early Church

v— *liturgy*. Ephesians, as we have noted, is replete with prayers, with doxologies, with material belonging to catechumenate instruction.

Apostolic foundation, unity of faith and doctrine, a creed, baptism, liturgy give definite shape to the Church of the first century as to the Church of all centuries.

## Recommended Readings

P. Benoit, "Body, Head and *Pleroma* in the Epistles of the Captivity," *Jesus and the Gospel*, Vol 2 (Seabury, 1974), 51-92. This is a magnificent treatment of Paul's doctrines of Body of Christ, Christ as head, Christ's fullness. Perhaps nothing better has ever been written on the subject. It emphasizes a strong realistic meaning in the term, Body of Christ. We are the Body of Christ because we are joined to Christ's risen body. Benoit, at least when this article was written in its original French in 1956, believed that Eph was written by a disciple of Paul who was directed by the apostle, and who utilized the recently completed letter to the Colossians.

K. Donfried, "Justification and Last Judgment in Paul, *Interpretation* 30 (1976), 140-152 discusses two important points: the relationship of justification, sanctification and salvation in Paul's theology. Salvation is future, but in a present process.

I. Havener, *1 Thess, Philippians, Philemon, 2 Thess, Colossians, Ephesians* (Liturgical Press: CBC #8, 1983) has a fine commenary on Eph directed to a lay audience. He believes that Eph was written by a Paulinist toward the end of the 1st century, and was meant to be a theological treatise in circular-letter form.

J. Houlden, *Paul's Letters from Prison: Philipians, Colossians, Philemon, and Ephesians* (Westminister, 1970) again presents an excellent commentary, readable and comprehensive. As an exegete he does fine work. He believes that Eph was written by a Christian leader some 30-50 years after Paul's death in the sixties.

J. Paul Sampley, "The Letter to the Ephesians," *Ephesians, Colossians, 2 Thess, The Pastoral Epistles* (Fortress: Proclamation, 1978), 9-39, offers an outstanding thematic treatment of Eph. Though not a commentary, it is a fine introduction. The epistle was written, not by Paul, but by a close follower who wrote in Paul's behalf.

L. Swain, *Ephesians* (Michael Glazier: NT Message #13, 1980). Swain has written an excellent commentary. Though it intends to be, and is, popular, it is also comprehensive. The author believes that Paul wrote the letter, but with greater latitude than usual given to his secretary. He also believes that Eph was a circular letter, destined for several churches, and written during Paul's Roman captivity, 61-63 AD.

# Epilogue

And so our journey through these ten Pauline letters has come to an end. It has been a long journey, but, I hope, neither boring nor disappointing. Reading Paul's letters means getting under his skin, getting into his head, getting into his heart. We have met the Paul who loves and cries, the Paul who anguishes for his people Israel and for his new Christians. We have come to know a Paul who becomes angry and ironic, but who also creates some of the most beautiful lyric passages known to humankind. Paul is in no way an antiseptic saint, living on a mountain top and summoning us out of the world to a life of monastic isolation. This Paul of Tarsus is eminently human and involved. Most of our own defects are duplicated in him, and this makes him approachable and real. In Paul we find no impeccable knight of the Table Round, but a manual worker taken over by the Lord and summoned to the Lord's work, commissioned by the risen Christ to be a light to the Gentiles, a light to the world. In this work he viewed himself as a weak instrument, as an earthen vessel, but in this work he was adamant and untiring. A sinner, a man subject to mistakes, a missioner hated by his beloved Jews and mistrusted by the Jerusalem Christians, he carried his burden to his death, as had the earthly Jesus of Nazareth. Hated by many, he was loved by a long list of people in whose lives he had been a powerful influence. He was loved by the men free and eager to share both his vision and his suffering. And he was loved by many women whose cooperation he appreciated and praised, and by whom he was supported and nourished. He was an extraordinary man, a genius in many ways. The first of the great Christian theologians to put his thoughts in writing, he has never been surpassed during the centuries that have followed. Apostle, evangelist, preacher, missionary, poet, he was above all, and at the bottom of it all, the servant of the risen Lord. In Christ he lived and moved and had his being. We rejoice in his friendship.